NEW EDITION

A STUDY OF
Twentieth-Century Harmony

(ÉTUDE SUR L'HARMONIE MODERNE)

A TREATISE AND GUIDE
FOR THE STUDENT-COMPOSER OF TO-DAY

BY

RENÉ LENORMAND, 1846-1932.

ENGLISH TRANSLATION BY

HERBERT ANTCLIFFE

With Preface by MOSCO CARNER

Volume One—HARMONY IN FRANCE TO 1914

Price, 7/6 net

LONDON: JOSEPH WILLIAMS, LIMITED

29 Enford Street, Marylebone, W.1

U.S.A.
THE B. F. WOOD MUSIC CO.
BOSTON

PARIS
"LE MONDE MUSICAL"
114 bis Boulevard Malesherbes

A COMPANION VOLUME
TO
RENÉ LENORMAND'S BOOK

A STUDY OF
Twentieth-Century Harmony
— Volume 2 —

BY

MOSCO CARNER

Contemporary Harmony

Price 6/- net

☛ *Copies can be ordered of the Publishers* ☛

TABLE OF CONTENTS

INDEX OF MUSICAL EXAMPLES

PREFACE TO THE NEW EDITION

THIS book first came out under the title "A Study of Modern Harmony." The facts, however, that it was written before the Great War (1914-1918), and is in the Author's own words "almost exclusively French in its scope" seemed to demand the adoption of a new title for the present republication, a title more precisely describing its actual scope. Thus the choice fell upon "Harmony in France to 1914."

French harmony of this period is essentially that of the so-called impressionistic composers with Debussy as their central figure. It is late in the day to stress again in detail the important place which the harmonic style of this school occupies in the evolution of modern harmony, not only in France but in other countries. During the first decade or so of our century there was hardly a musical nation in Europe—and this applies also to a great number of composers in North and South America—that was not in varying degrees influenced by the French impressionists. It was the last occasion in the history of music that the individual style of a national school was so generally accepted in other countries.

A complete technical study of musical impressionism in France would have, of course, to include a number of phenomena besides harmony. Nevertheless, harmony is unquestionably the most interesting aspect of impressionism. For although the ground was already prepared on the one hand by the later German romantics, notably Wagner, and on the other hand by some of the Russian writers of the nineteenth century, the harmonic inventions and changes of the French impressionists were so many and so far-reaching that they imperatively demand special and separate study.

A few words about the Author and his method. René Lenormand (1846-1932) belonged to the same generation as Fauré, Chabrier and Duparc. He was primarily known as a song writer and composer of chamber music. He also founded and directed the society *Le Lied en Tous Pays* which had for its object the presentation in France of songs from all countries. Lenormand did not set out in his book to

iii

propound a theory or give a dissertation on French impressionistic harmony. His purpose was in the main a practical one. It was to show the student-composer by a number of typical passages the various new devices and treatments of chords as employed by his French contemporaries. His book is a sort of *catalogue raisonné* which, if it does not give the underlying. idea of all the harmonic phenomena of his time, has the advantage of marshalling them in a comprehensive order. It goes without saying that the views expressed in this book necessarily differ from our present-day notions. After all what seemed so new and revolutionary at the beginning of our century has in the light of later experiences become a matter of course, and lost its appeal of novelty. This, however, does not in the least detract from the value of Lenormand's study, in which perhaps an additional interest will be found by comparing his views with our ideas on the subject. This, incidentally, was the main reason for republishing the book in its original, unaltered form.

Important as the harmonic writing of the French impressionists is, it represents only a part of the evolution of modern harmony. The writer of this preface has, therefore, issued, at the request of the publishers a sequel to the book dealing with the general development of Contemporary Harmony in other countries from 1914 onwards. It is thus hoped to give the student-composer a comprehensive survey of all the various devices which have combined to make twentieth-century harmony such a complicated and fascinating study.

MOSCO CARNER.

PREFACE

As human sensibility modifies itself ceaselessly during the course of the centuries, Music, its faithful interpreter, evolves side by side with it.*

A deep study of the continual transformations of the musical art would be out of place in this work, which is of an essentially modern character. We leave on one side the music of the Ancient Greeks, and also that of the Middle Ages, and consider only the great evolution of the seventeenth century.** This laid the foundations of the musical theory still used in our own days, and in its results, is of the highest importance. It was this that made possible the brilliant achievements of the 18th and 19th centuries.

Whether they wish it or not, all those who think musically are more or less impregnated with the idioms of that phase of the art.

But the page on which are inscribed the illustrious names of Bach, Mozart, Beethoven, Schumann, Wagner, etc., has scarcely been turned, when already new formulas appear.

The result of this state of things is that young musicians learn the practice of their art following the rules of the older technique, and then find themselves out of their bearings when they would write in the modern style; from which it arises that they fall into exaggerations for lack of the instruction appropriate to contemporary musical thought.

"But," say the theorists, "the teaching which we hold rests on immutable bases." This assertion is disputable. Is it not a little dangerous to speak of the immutability of a

---

* In our days this evolution proceeds so rapidly that a composer, arrived at the close of his career, has the sadness of being no longer in communion of idea with the young composers, unless he has kept his mind open to the constant transformation of the art. It is a curious fact that the majority of the elder musicians take sides against the new forms. Sincere and true artists — they are that, surely — should, it would seem, take a passionate interest in the evolution of the art. But these conclude, doubtless, that their works mark a definite, irrevocable condition.

** Evolution commencing from the 16th century.

system which relies on an artificial scale? At the present time this system consists of thirty-one sounds comprised within the compass of an octave. As a matter of fact these thirty-one sounds are reduced to twelve by the convention of *temperament.**

---

* Although the system of temperament may be known to all, we think it may be useful to recall it. If, starting from a G♭♭, a series of rigorously exact ascending 5ths is built up, the 31 actual sounds which constitute our system will be obtained. The whole of the "Traité d'harmonie" of Gevaert (published by Lemoine) is based on that series of fifths. Whatever may be the note taken as the point of departure, at the twelfth successive fifth it will be perceived that the sounds no longer agree with the octave; so that in bringing these 31 sounds within the compass of the octave none is the equisonant of the other (see Fig. I). There has thus been made a compromise or mean in order to have but twelve sounds to the octave (Fig. II). This convention, which was made scientifically about 1700, has been called *tuning by equal temperament.* Guido d'Arezzo must have practised temperament, but it was not until later that Mersennus and afterwards Loulié and Sauveur put forward some scientific explanations. Rameau brought these to a more perfect development about 1720 in order afterwards to devote himself to the study of harmonics (Fig. III).

Fig. I.	Fig. II.	Fig. III.
Theoretical system. (31 sounds.)	Practical system. (12 sounds.)	Natural sounds. (First harmonics.)

In other words, we write music as if we had thirty-one sounds at our disposal, and we execute it by means of twelve sounds.

At the present time composers content themselves with a rejuvenation of the classical theory. It may be a day will come when they will weary of the false combination in which conception and execution are different one from the other.* But then, on which side will they find themselves?

Continuing to accept the thirty-one sounds and repudiating the *temperament,* will they demand untempered instruments? That would be logical, but it would revolutionise the manufacture of instruments.

In the above table (Fig. I) we represent the relative pitch of the different sounds according to the feeling of musicians, but while these maintain that C♯, for example, is higher than D♭, the physicists affirm the contrary. This contradiction may perhaps be explained if we admit that the semitone resulting from the calculation of the physicists has not the same origin as that of the musicians.

In the bulletin No. 2 (1908) of the Institut Psychologique, M. Jean Marnold has made an interesting communication as to the possibility of bringing the musician and the physicist into agreement. Incidentally he reproaches composers for their ignorance in the matter of acoustics. Perhaps they are wrong in taking too little interest in this question; but what can they do, if it is not to be connected with *temperament,* while waiting for the theorists to understand each other sufficiently to give them a logical system *in which theory and practice shall be in agreement?*

* Musicians who play instruments with variable sounds justify themselves by saying: "We do not play the tempered notes; we play the music as it is written." This is perhaps true of the string quartet, or any other groups not comprising instruments with fixed sounds, but it is very highly contestable whenever the two kinds are used in combination. An orchestra, when it accompanies a concerto for the piano — an instrument with fixed sounds — is compelled to play tempered sounds if it does not wish to play out of tune.

Besides, an orchestra comprises some instruments of fixed sounds; if some artists were to play the Pythagorean sounds, as they claim, the others playing the tempered sounds, the effect would be very disagreeable; while if a third class of instrumentalists played the natural sounds it would result in incredible discord. The imperfection of the auditory organ of some would, perhaps, enable them to bear it, but reason could not allow it. And as for Chamber music with the piano; would composers and virtuosos who have passed their lives composing and playing music for piano and string instruments really have borne this continual dissonance, if it had been actually produced? And Vocal music! In his "Principes du Système musical et de l'Harmonie" (J. Hamelle), M. Anselme Vinée says: "Contrary to a common opinion it is physiologically impossible for the voice, accompanied by an instrument of unchangeable sounds, to emit tempered intervals. When its natural intonation leads to a sound in discord with the note fixed at the moment, a union must quickly be produced, but always by flexion." Without entering into the learned considerations of M. Vinée (see his treatise, pp. 41 and 64), it suffices in the present case that we state the fact of this union.

Will they shape their thought to the scale of natural sounds, with its harmonics not included in the present system? The attempt has just been made.*

Will they adopt, in theory, the division of the octave into twelve equal semitones, as it in practice exists for instruments with fixed sounds? That would not change the sound of the music, but would modify the theory and banish the accidental signs ♯, ♭ and ♮.** This would be the end of the system of thirty-one sounds, and also of *temperament*.

In any case, it is impossible that theoretical music and practical music will not end by coming into agreement with each other. One can foresee that this will not be done without severe struggles. "The time has not yet arrived" say the professors; "one must learn one's trade well with the

---

For us, although the voice and the instruments with variable sounds can execute the thirty-one sounds of our theoretical system, it seems proved that as soon as an instrument of fixed sounds is heard simultaneously with them, all artists, instinctively, sing and play the tempered note :—that is, as we have said before, interpret through the medium of twelve notes that which is written for thirty-one notes. That statement, carefully checked, would be of great importance to the partisans of the theoretical division of the scale into twelve equal spaces.

*.The Russian composer, Scriabine, in his "Prometheus" for orchestra, has just written the novel scale
              C, D, E, F♯, A, B♭.
formed of the 8th, 9th, 10th, 11th, 13th and 14th harmonics (see Fig. 3, page vi); the orchestra does not play the tempered sounds, it plays the natural sounds by taking count of the actual pitch of numbers 11, 13, and 14. "Musique à Moscou"; Nicolas Petroff; *Monde Musical;* 30th June 1911.

** In the "Cours de Composition Musicale," of M. Vincent d'Indy (Vol. I, 1902, Durand), his collaborator, M. Auguste Sèrieyx, gives in a note (p. 62) some personal ideas on the suppression of the accidental signs (♯, ♭, ♮), by the employment of a staff of which each degree (line or space) represents invariably a tempered semitone.

More recently, M. Menchaca, an Argentine theorist, has brought forward a system of notation, which we cannot explain here, but the result of which is the division of the octave into twelve equal intervals.

The names chosen by M. Menchaca for his scale of twelve degrees are: do, dou, re, ro, mi, fa, fe, sol, nou, la, se, si. Some of these may be replaced with advantage, for they seem to suggest a certain relation between the notes, which, under these conditions ought not to exist. This theorist himself makes the observation that a certain number of vibrations produces a fixed sound, and that there is no reason for connecting that sound with its neighbours. "Each sound is or is not; it has a physical existence which cannot be modified." "Système Musical Menchaca" (Pleyel, Lyon & Co.). The scale of twelve degrees suppresses the accidental signs: "The ♯ and the ♭ are of all known musical characters the most vexatiously conventional."

The first difficulty to be overcome, if a change of system is to be arrived at, will be to find a mode of notation for this scale of twelve degrees — that of M. Menchaca would appear to be difficult of application to polyphonic music. The problem does not appear to be insoluble, and we know that on many sides attempts are being made to solve it.

present system." Without doubt, but it is to be wished
that it should be done under such conditions that once the
studies are completed the creative faculty shall not be
forced into a groove.*

In matters of art it is dangerous to learn to do as others
do. Certainly it is necessary to consult tradition in order
to interpret the masterpieces of the past; but to invoke
tradition when it is a question of creating — is not that a
false way which can only lead to a plagiarising of one's
predecessors?

To return to Modern Harmony: that which makes the new
school particularly interesting is the considerable effort it is
making to free itself from the laws of the older technique
without having any other guide save the intuition of a new
idea of beauty. Certain authors — and this is a widespread
idea in the world of amateurs — imagine that in these days
one can write "no matter what." They misunderstand the
character of the evolution of to-day. The most daring composers are all technicians of the greatest ability.** Those
who unite to such mastery the greater gift of a truly musical temperament bring themselves naturally to the first
rank. The others, complicating the harmony simply with
the pleasure of the grammarian, class themselves rather
among the theorists than among the creators, which nevertheless assures them an important place.

The harmony called *modern*, considered as a means of
technique does not suffice to constitute *a modern music*.
Such compositions, where are to be found gathered together
all the new devices, often give only a negative impression.
On the other hand, some works based on harmonies relatively simple can invoke an intensely modern atmosphere.***
Above the manner of writing there is, therefore, *the modern
inspiration*, and the musicians of classical education make a
mistake when they complicate their harmonies thinking

---

* A composer very much to the front, who belongs to the modern
school, declares that he himself has found several years of desperate
effort necessary to get rid of the impressions received in the time of his
studentship, and to re-establish his individuality.

** We speak of serious and well-instructed artists, leaving on one
side the crowd of imitators, with whom the search after strange and
weird harmonies only serves to hide their ignorance and absolute lack
of musicality.

*** There are to be found many examples in the music of M. Gabriel
Fauré, who, by the peculiar and charming turn he gives to some harmonic combinations, which are relatively little complicated, is one of
the most modern composers of our epoch. The precursor of the movement of to-day, with which he still remains associated by his productions, his position in the history of French music will be important.

thus to modernise themselves. Before all else they must write with the sincerity of their inspiration and of their feeling.

The composers who, about forty years ago, contributed to the evolution of the art with all the ardour of their youth, fulfilled their duty at a useful time. Present-day masters maintain an obstinate struggle for the acceptance of the new formulas which are imposed on them by the inevitable transformation of all things — an irresistible force to which they are compelled to submit. One may overwhelm them by comparing their works with those of the masters of the past; but the question is not one of knowing whether they are doing better or worse than their predecessors. Their mission as composers, that is, *inventors*, of music, is to manifest their sensibility in a new language, to write something other than that which has already been written.

The new school* makes itself known by works of a peculiar charm, which are not without some affinity with other more pretentious and unmusical productions. Must there be seen in these only a refinement of the older art, or are they to be considered as the beginning of a new art? It is difficult to foresee the answer which our descendants will make to these two questions.** As to those who imagine that a return will be made to the past, or who think that a new genius will be brought to light through the medium of the technique and æsthetic of the past, their illusion, we believe, is complete. There can no more be a new Beethoven than there can be a new Christopher Columbus.

While waiting for the didactic work which will build up, it may be, a new musical system, it has seemed to us interesting to extract some of the most typical harmonic examples that we have met with in the works of modern authors. We must ask the young harmonist who may read this little book to consider it as a document of transition between the treatises of the past and those of the future, as a sort of inventory of modern harmony; as a landmark planted in a vast field of sonorous vibrations which musicians have been indefatigably clearing for more than twenty-five centuries.

RENÉ LENORMAND.***

---

* By the audacity of his harmonies and also by their charm and musicality, M. Debussy may be considered as the chief of this school. Doubtless he had his precursors, he has his emulators, he will have his successors; but the score of "Pelleas et Melisande" marks an epoch in the history of the art.

** See Chap. XII. Conclusions.

*** I owe an explanation to those of my friends who may be surprised at the tendencies of this publication. I am going to give it them, and in so doing must apologise for speaking of myself. It is absurd to suppose that musical evolution can stand still at any moment whatever of its history; and there is no reason for a composer, whatever may be his age, or whatever his production, to show himself indifferent or hostile to that evolution. But neither that which is nor that which shall be can destroy that which has been. I have therefore been able to write this little work without abandoning anything of my profound admiration for the Masters of the past, and without abjuring any of my productions which, good or bad, remain the sincere expression of a feeling which time has been able to modify.

R. L.

EXPLANATORY NOTES

In order not to multiply beyond measure the number of our quotations, we had intended to confine our choice to the most typical examples met with in works themselves considered as typical. On consideration, we have adopted the plan of consulting a large number of works in order to evoke more completely the "atmosphere" in which the modern French school lives and moves.

Here in alphabetical order is a list of composers whose works are quoted:

MM. Louis Aubert, Alfred Bruneau, Caplet, E. Chabrier, E. Chausson, Claude Debussy, Paul Dukas, Gabriel Dupont, Fanelli, Gabriel Fauré, Alexandre Georges, Jean Huré, Vincent d'Indy, Charles Koechlin, René Lenormand, Ernest Moret, Léon Moreau, Maurice Ravel, Albert Roussel, Samuel Rousseau, Saint-Saëns, Erik Satie, Florent Schmitt, Déodat de Sévérac and Woollett.

As will be seen by this list, this little book is almost exclusively French in its scope.

It goes without saying that we are concerned only with harmonic facts, or with modes of writing which present a modern feeling.

We have no intention of proposing a new system or of writing a treatise on harmony; we present merely a collection of examples which we have explained as far as possible through the medium of the earlier technique.* ̄

---

* In order to reckon with some of the processes of the modern school it will be well to refer to the harmonic series:

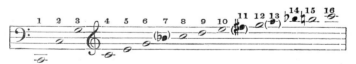

Here will be found, we believe, the origin of a certain number of progressions reproved by classical teaching.

Some of the authors quoted have willingly helped us to make a *précis* of their intentions, and to them we present our sincere thanks. If in these notes the celebrated names of MM. Massenet, Dubois, etc., etc., are not met with, it is that these masters, of an indisputable talent, have doubtless judged that the harmonic innovations with which we

---

In no case must any too definite statements be based on the harmonic series, because, not only do the sounds 7, 11 and 13 lack preciseness, but the whole series may be found to be modified by the manner in which the sounding body is set in vibration.

The harmonic series has been requisitioned in all possible fashions; from it have been deduced a number of systems more or less ingenious, more or less erroneous. We will add nothing to these labours of physicists who surpass us in competence, but limit ourselves to a simple deduction which is to be found formulated in Chapter II and also, partially, in Chapter I.

It may not be useless, and in any case it will be interesting, to run through the different systems that sprang up after Rameau. Here are the names of the authors of *some* of these treatises: — Marpurg, Testori, the Abbé Roussier, Levens, Sorge, Père Valloti, Père Sabbatini, the Abbé Vogler, Knecht, Daube, Schroeter, Kirnberger, Gottfried Weber, Derode, Langlé, Reicha, Berton, Catel, de Momigny, Blein, Schneider, Jelensperger, Fétis, etc., etc. We stop this list about the middle of the 19th century, at which period appeared the treatises known to all. The name of Rameau dominates this enormous effort; his theories were the origin of all these frequently contradictory systems, and remained in use until the coming of Catel.

And looking over these older works several interesting names are encountered: —Père Sabbatini among others, who after having worked with Père Martini placed himself under the direction of Père Valotti, Maestro di Cappella at St. Anthony's, Padua. Valotti published only the first part of his treatise (*Della Scienza Teorica e practica della Moderna Musica*, libro primo, in Padova 1779) and it was Sabbatini who formulated the harmonies of his master. They did not fail of a certain modern savour as may be judged by the following: —

To the common chord he added the 9th and presented it thus:

We may notice that the common chord with the 9th added — it is not a chord of the 9th — is often to be met with in the modern school (Chap. IV [9]). It may be analysed as an appoggiatura sounded against the harmony-note.

To the common chord he added also the 11th, which may be analysed like the preceding: i.e., as an appoggiatura sounded at the same time as the harmony-note.

are concerned, were contrary to their æsthetic principles, and, save with rare exceptions, they have not employed them.

Père Sabbatini — coming at least two centuries too soon — stated that the inversion of a 9th was a 7th. So, the modern school frequently employs the 9th below the root in inversions of chords of the 9th (Chap. III [14]). They use even the 4th inversion of the chord of the 9th, pronounced impracticable by the classical theorists. (Chap. III [11] Chap. XI [19]).

TWO OR MORE CONSECUTIVE FIFTHS

By Similar and Conjunct Motion

These are forbidden, say the treatises of harmony in use to-day. They do not explain why a composer should not write two or more consecutive fifths in similar and conjunct motion, if these fifths correspond with a musical intention which cannot be realised without their occurrence.

It seems that the feeling of repose evoked by that interval, which requires nothing after it, must secure it against any very free movement. Without attaching too much importance to the fact, it is not without use to remember that the 5th is the 3rd of the harmonic series. Thus, a somewhat refined ear can distinguish quite clearly the 3rd harmonic; consequently each time that a composer sounds two notes on conjunct degrees, he sounds at the same time two consecutive fifths by similar and conjunct motion:

This is an "indication" that is not without value, relative to the possibility of using fifths with the bass. There should be no confusion of the natural harmonic of which we speak with the artificial harmonics of the mutation stops of the organ.

* * *

Besides, fifths have always been written:

Melody in the Dorian mode — ancient Greek — accompanied by the upper fifth : *Traité d'harmonie* by Gevaert (Lemoine, publisher).

In the middle ages all the chants and melodies were accompanied at the fifth or at the fourth; the different combinations which they formed were designated by the general name of *Organum*. On this subject Hucbald wrote with enthusiasm: "You will see a suave harmony born of this combination."*

Organum
at the 5th

Nos qui vi - vi-mus be -ne- di- ci- mus Do- mi-num

Organum
at the 4th

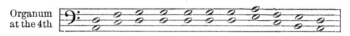

Tu   pa - tris sem - pi - ter - nus es   fi - li - us

Little by little consecutive fifths were abandoned, and at the commencement of the 14th century we find them forbidden by Jean de Muris. We must say that Gevaert has attributed their first prohibition to Tinctoris in the 15th century. Nevertheless, Jean de Muris is very explicit with regard to successive fifths.

* * *

The masters of the period which immediately preceded our own have carefully avoided them. Nevertheless, there are few authors in whose works some are not to be met with.

---

* *Histoire de la Musique Moderne*, Marcillac (Fischbacher).

** Kiesewetter has disputed the practical existence of Organum, seeing in it only an aberration of the theorist. *Geschichte der europæisch-abendliechen or unsrer heutigen Musik*, 2nd ed. (Leipsic). From all the evidence it appears that he was mistaken, and that successions of fifths were in use in the Middle Ages.

In the country churches, when the faithful sing in unison, it often happens that some among them accompany the women's voices a 4th below and the men's voices a 5th above; that is the old *Organum*. M. Lavignac has noticed, as we have, and has justly remarked (*La Musique et les Musiciens*, Delagrave), that the fifth and the fourth are the intervals which most resemble the octave: octave $\frac{2}{1}$, fifth $\frac{3}{2}$, fourth $\frac{4}{3}$.

It is probable that these peasants, lacking musical education, imagined themselves singing at the octave or unison with the other voices.

We may quote the following examples:

ROSSINI. *William Tell.* (2nd Act.)

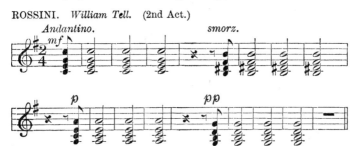

BEETHOVEN. *Eroica Symphony.* (1st movement.)

It is interesting to note the care that Beethoven has taken to allow the recollection of each fifth to be lost before attacking another.

SCHUMANN, Op. 26. *Finale.*

Here are some fragments of modern works. The successions of fifths here are used under the conditions which are summarised at the end of the chapter.

CLAUDE DEBUSSY. *Chansons de Bilitis.* (Fromont, Pubr.)

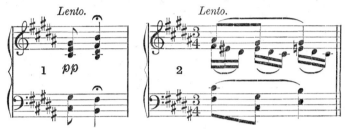

(1) *Lento:* The 5th doubled, proceeds by contrary motion.
(2) *Lento:* Several consecutive fifths by disjunct motion.

Study of Modern Harmony.

(3) (4) (5) (6) See the "Deductions" page 11.

CH. KOECHLIN.   *Les rêves morts.* Op. 13, No. 2.
L'astre rouge. Op. 13.   (Rouart & Lerolle, Pubr.)

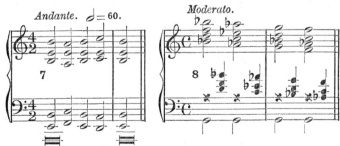

(7) Fifths between the inner parts, with contrary motion of the upper part.
(8) Fifths between the inner parts.

ALEXANDRE GEORGES. *Hymne au soleil.* (Enoch, Pubr.)

(9) Chromatic fifths.

SAMUEL ROUSSEAU. *La Cloche du Rhin* (1898). Page 11.

(Choudens, Pubr.)

(10) Fifths by Chromatic steps; the 3rd is common to the two chords.

G. FAURÉ. *Le Secret.*   *Prison.*   (J. Hamelle, Pubr.)

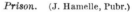

(11) Fifths with similar motion in all the parts.
(12) Fifths between the outer parts with similar motion in all the parts.

SAINT–SAËNS.   *5th Pianoforte Concerto.*   (Durand, Pubr.)

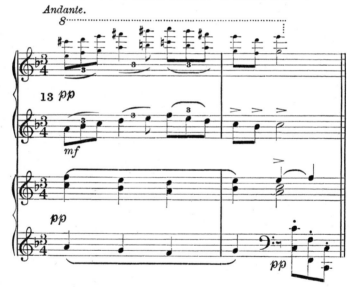

(13) In performance the listener cannot but notice an imitation of percussion instruments used in the East. Organists who have taken part in performances of the Oratorios and Cantatas of Handel and Bach, under the direction of Gevaert, know that erudite musician forbade the use of mutation stops, finding that the artificial harmonics conflicted with the natural harmonics of the Orchestra. The use which M. Saint-Saëns makes of them on the piano (sounds 3 & 5) is both original and piquant.

DÉODAT de SÉVERAC. *Un rêve.* (Edition mutuelle.)

(14) Fifths between the lower parts, with oblique motion of an inner part.

RENÉ LENORMAND. *Pièces exotiques.* (J. Hamelle, Pubr.)

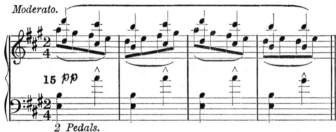

(15) Fifths caused by the melodic outline; contained within the limits of the octave.

E. MORET. *Préludes,* (*No. 9*). (Heugel, Pubr.)

(16) Chord of the 6th and 3rd arranged so that the 3rd is above the 6th, which causes the fifth between the two upper parts.

E. MORET.   *Interlude.   Impression de neige.*   (Heugel, Pubr.)

(17) Continued in the same manner for several bars. The fifths here do not result from the progression of the parts in the harmonic tissue. It is a melody accompanied by the fifth continuously. The sound of the same interval indefinitely repeated causes monotony. In the present case, *Impression de neige,* the effect is intended by the author, and the fifths evoke effectively the sombre melancholy of a snowy day.

CLAUDE DEBUSSY.   *Hommage à Rameau.*   (Durand, (Pubr.)

(18)   etc.   See the Deductions, page 11, No. 3.

RENÉ LENORMAND. *Le voyage imaginaire — Chapelle bretonne,*
(1889). (J. Hamelle, Pubr.)

(19) Fifths between the lower parts.

H. WOOLLETT. *La neige.* (Hamelle, Pubr.)

(20) Fifths in two octaves, with similar motion in all parts.

ALEXANDRE GEORGES. *Miarka.* Page 255. (Enoch, Pubr.)

(21) Fifths by semitones
between the outer parts.

A. BRUNEAU. *Le Rêve* (1891). (Choudens, Pubr.)

(22) Fifths by disjunct motion, with notes in common between the
chords.

page 9.

(23) Fifths with the bass, duplicated in other parts.

SAINT–SAËNS.   *Le Pas d'Armes du Roi Jean.*   (Durand, Pubr.)
  Animato.

Moi-nes, Vier-ges Por - te - ront De grands cierges Sur son front

(24) This work was composed in 1852 (when the composer was 17 years of age) and published in 1855.   The fifths are intended to give an impression of bells.

DEDUCTIONS

Without any intention of formulating new rules, we may, by generalising from the foregoing instances, deduce the following indications having special relation to the modern style.

(1). Two or more fifths in succession, in similar and conjunct motion, are readily used in the two lowest parts,* where the upper parts proceed by contrary or oblique motion. (1), (10), (14).

(2). They are also used in the two lowest parts, accompanied by similar motion in all the parts. These successions of fifths are generally short, and will be so much the better if some precautions are taken as to the mode of approaching and leaving them, e.g. : —

(i.) The last fifth approached by disjunct motion with a note in common between the chords. (3), (5).

(ii.) The fifths proceeding by similar and conjunct motion, the last fifth accompanied by some contrary motion in the upper part. (4), (6).

(iii.) Successions of fifths which terminate by similar motion are met with; but they are more rarely found.

(3). Used in the upper parts they may be presented in two ways: —

(i.) Bare fifths (16), (17). They are thus very prominent, and a number cannot be heard in succession without monotony. In alternation with other intervals that effect is modified. (11), (15).

---

* Classical teaching admits the possibility of certain fifths by semitone.

TH. DUBOIS. *Notes et études d'harmonie.* Page 97. (Heugel, Pubr.)

("Tolerable, even for the student, by placing them in the lowest parts.") (Th. Dubois).

This work completes the "Traité de Reber," and one or other may always be consulted for everything which relates to classical technique.

(ii.) If the third is added, a succession of chords of three notes in root position is given; the adding of the lower octave of the fifth gives a chord of a disposition specially suited to the pianoforte, and of great sonority. (18).

(4). Fifths are of good effect in the inner parts, particularly when they are associated with contrary motion in the other parts. (7) If they result from chords of the 6th and 3rd with the parts doubled (a combination practised for many years), they lose some of their character. (8).

(5). They are more rarely used between the extreme parts by similar motion in all the parts. (12), (21).

(6). By disjunct motion they are readily used with notes in common between the chords. (2), (22).

(7). Chromatic fifths may be freely used. (9), (21).

(8). If a long succession of fifths is given in the lower parts, they cease to form a part of the harmonic tissue. (19), (20), (23).

(9). They may always be used where the composer has a definite aim (13), (15), (22); but they are still forbidden whenever they are the result of awkwardness or lack of skill in writing; a prohibition, moreover, which may be applied to any interval whatever.

CHAPTER II

CHORDS OF THE SEVENTH

One knows that by resolving a chord of the seventh on a chord a fifth below, what is called the natural resolution is obtained. Under the name of exceptional resolutions many others are used, either by retaining the seventh, or by making it rise or fall by conjunct degrees, and proceeding to any other chord but that of a fifth below. We find the "recipe" for these resolutions in all treatises on Harmony.

The modern school has further enlarged the circle of these resolutions by making chords of the seventh move by similar and conjunct motion in all parts, ascending or descending. We may add that, usual or exceptional, these resolutions may be made by interchange of parts. As we shall see, all modern authors write these successions.*

---

* These resolutions may find their origin, if not their justification, in the succession of two notes by conjunct motion. Taking for example, the sound of C; we have the first harmonics as follows:

Thus, a practised ear will distinguish the odd harmonics, 3, 5 and 7, as those which give the following chord of the 7th

making some reservation as to the just intonation of the sound No. 7.

If after the note C, we sound that of D, it produces a new series of harmonics:

EXAMPLES

G. FAURÉ.   *Le parfum impérissable.*   (J. Hamelle, Pubr.)

Andante.

(1) Succession by conjunct motion, descending, of two third-inversions of the chord of the ⁊*

---

* The small + always indicates the presence of the leading note. (Translator.)

This gives us a new chord of the 7th (with the same reservation for the sound No. 7).

The D coming immediately after the C, the first chord is succeeded by the second by similar and conjunct motion in all the parts:

Modern composers may, therefore, allege that they do nothing but work in the mould which Nature indicates to them.   It is an indication that is not easily seen, it is true, but of which, nevertheless, account may be taken.

If, continuing to accept the sound 7 as a minor 7th, the harmonic ninth is added, a succession of chords of the 9th will be obtained by conjunct degrees:

E. CHAUSSON.   *Serres chaudes.*   Page 6.   (Rouart et Lerolle, Pubr.)

(2) Chords of the 7th by conjunct motion. They may also be analysed as, (*a*) ornamentation of the 3rd, 5th and 7th, the succession of two chords of the 7th, however, remaining.

SAMUEL ROUSSEAU.   *La cloche du Rhin.*   Page 135.

(Choudens, Pubr.)

It may be objected that if several notes are heard simultaneously, they produce so many series of harmonics that the mixture reduces the importance of the above deductions. That is true, and therefore, we give them only as a theoretical suggestion.

(3) (*a*) (*b*) Chords of the 7th by conjunct degrees. (*b*) E is an appoggiatura. (*c*) Change of the chord on the resolution of the appoggiatura. (E♯ for F.)

Andantino.   page 201.

(4) Second inversions of the chord of ♈ moving by conjunct degrees and similar motion in all the parts.

page 138.

(5) Successions of second inversions of chords of the 7th by conjunct and similar motion in all the parts. The presence of the 9th in the upper part does not alter the character of the succession.

page 59. *8va*..

Passing chords.

page 88.

(7) Succession of chords of the 7th of the 3rd species* by semitones and similar movement in all the parts under an inverted pedal.

page 68.   *(c)*

(8)   (*a*)   Chords of the 7th by conjunct degrees.
      (*b*)   Resolution by interchange of parts.
      (*c*)   Alteration of the 5th.

A. BRUNEAU.   *Messidor.*   Page 211.   (Choudens, Pubr.)

(9) Succession of chords of the 7th by conjunct degrees, (*b*) becoming the chord of the 9th at (*c*).

We may also say that this is a chord of E minor succeeded by the chord of the 9th on G, with passing notes in the bass; but the pause on C♯ gives it the character of a chord of the seventh, and, when it is followed by the chord of the seventh on B, two chords of the seventh are heard by conjunct motion.

---

* (Translator's note: This method of numbering the Species of Chords will be explained by reference to example (22) in this Chapter.)

G. FAURÉ.   *Le parfum impérissable.*   (J. Hamelle, Pubr.)

(10) Resolution by interchange of parts.

(10²) A peculiar charm resulting from the very free movement of the parts.

G. FAURÉ.   *Adieu.*   (Durand, Pubr.)

(11) Resolution by interchange of parts.

G. FAURÉ.   *Le secret.*   *Au cimetière.*   (J. Hamelle, Pubr.)

(12) Resolution by interchange of parts.
(12²) Resolution by interchange of parts.

E. CHABRIER.   *Le roi malgré lui.*   (Enoch, Pubr.)

page 52.

(13)   1st inversions of the chords of the 7th, moving by step.

LÉON MOREAU.   *Dans la nuit.*   (Pfister, Pubr.)

(14)   Successions of the second inversion of chords of the seventh.

Study of Modern Harmony.

Allegro.

(15)   Chord of the 7th of the 4th species mixed with the other species.

Study of Modern Harmony.

Très lent.

(16) Chords of the 7th of the first species by similar and conjunct motion in all the parts.*   There are to be found in Chopin and Schumann some successions of chords of the 7th moving by step.

CHABRIER.   *Briséis.*   Page 28.   (Enoch, Pubr.)

(17) Successions of the first inversion of chords of the 7th of the first species.

* It will be useful to recall here the close of the 21st Mazurka of Chopin; —

CLAUDE DEBUSSY. *Pelléas et Mélisande.* (Durand, Pubr.)

Et voi - ci des traces de sang.

(18) Successions of the 3rd inversion of the chord of the 7th of the 1st species with altered 5th.

Oh ! . . . ces pe-ti-tes mains.

(19) Succession of the 4th inversion of chords of the 7th by conjunct degrees (see previous note).

---

and also this bar of Schumann, *Scherzino* Op. 26, No. 3.

(20) Successions of 3rd inversions of various kinds on a pedal.

CLAUDE DEBUSSY.   *Pelléas et Mélisande.*   Durand, Pubr.)

(21) Successions of chords of the 7th of the 3rd species by conjunct degrees.

page 114.

(22) Successions of inversions of the four species of chords of the 7th.

page 10. *Animé.*

(23) Chord of the 7th with the 6th replacing the 5th.

The minor 6th having the same sound as the augmented 5th we can analyse the chord as a chord of the 7 with augmented 5th. This example finds a place here only for the purpose of showing the cause of No. 6 of the Deductions.

A. BRUNEAU. *Messidor.* Page 280. (Choudens, Pubr.)

(24) Succession of two chords of the 7th by conjunct motion of the bass and of the 7th, but with two notes in common; we mention this because of the movement of the two sevenths.

M. RAVEL.   *Sur l'herbe.*   (Durand, Pubr.)

Cevin de Chypre est exquis

(25)   (*a*) Inversions of the chords of the 7th moving by semitones.
       (*b*) Passing note.
       (*c*) G is an appoggiatura.
       (*d*) Pedal.

G. FAURÉ.   *La bonne Chanson.*   No. 5.   (J. Hamelle, Pubr.)

CLAUDE DEBUSSY.   *Pelléas et Mélisande.*   Page 26.   (Durand, Pubr.)

(27) Chords of the 7th of the 1st species, moving by conjunct and similar motion, with an inverted pedal, which note is an integral part of all the chords.

CLAUDE DEBUSSY. *Pelléas et Mélisande.* Page 204. (Durand, Pubr.)

(28) Succession of chords of the 7th of the 3rd species, moving by step.

DEDUCTIONS

We cannot repeat too often that we have no intention of formulating the rules of a new technique. In saying that modern composers use successions of chords of the seventh under the following conditions, we limit ourselves to observed facts.

(1). Two or more chords of the seventh of the first species may proceed by step (either of a tone or a semitone) and by similar motion in all the parts, ascending or descending, either in root position or in their inversions. (1), (3), (5), (13), (14), (16), (17), (26), (27).

(2). Chords of the seventh of the second species, whilst they may proceed under the same conditions as those of the first species, do not give so satisfying an impression. The more they are associated with other species the better they sound. (15), (19), (22), (24).

(3). Chords of the seventh of the third species are used under the same conditions as chords of the diminished seventh. (2), (6), (7), (9), (21), (28).

(4). The first inversion of the chord of the seventh of the fourth species lends itself better than other positions of that chord to successions by conjunct and similar motion — particularly by step of a semitone. Nevertheless, mixed with other species, it is used, as they are, in the root position as well as inverted. (15), (19), (22).

(5). In all the foregoing successions it must be noticed that the disposition of the parts plays an important *rôle*. In the inversions, the interval of the seventh is preferred to that of the second, although that arrangement may be practicable. (13), (25).

(6). Chords of the seventh with an augmentation of the fifth may proceed, in descending, by similar and conjunct motion. (18).

As the augmented fifth is the enharmonic of the minor sixth, these intervals are often written interchangeably. (23).

(7). Resolutions by interchange of parts are readily used. It suffices that the note of resolution be heard in any one of the parts whatsoever. (10), (11), (12).

CHAPTER III

CHORDS OF THE NINTH⸱

Chords of the ninth have, like chords of the seventh, their natural resolutions and those called exceptional. Both are found in all treatises on harmony, and have been exploited by all composers. We will concern ourselves now only with the resolutions which belong to the modern school, viz.: the succession of two chords of the ninth moving by step and in similar motion in all the parts.** We will add to these several resolutions little used in the classical technique.

The resolution of the ninth upon another such ninth by conjunct movement offends the sensibilities of many musicians; it is certain that two bare ninths in succession are unpleasant; but they are not at all disagreeable, and the ear accepts them readily, if the complete chord of the ninth is used, as it occurs in the harmonic series:

In all the successions which follow, the disposition of the parts is very important.

---

* The French treatises of Reber-Dubois and of Durand recognise but one chord of the ninth (major or minor). M. Gevaert in his "Traité d'harmonie" (Lemoine, Publisher), has admitted four species:

Chords of the 9th of 1st Species		Chords of the 9th of 2nd Species		Chords of the 9th of the 3rd Species.	Chords of the 9th of the 4th species.
with major ninth.	with minor ninth.	with major ninth.	with minor ninth.		

** See Chapter **II**, Chords of the Seventh, notes on the harmonic series.

EXAMPLES

G. FAURÉ.   *Prison.*   (J. Hamelle, Pubr., 1891.)
   Quasi adagio.

(1) Succession of two chords of the major 9th of the first species, moving by the descent of a major 2nd.

G. FAURÉ.   *La bonne Chanson.*   (J. Hamelle, Pubr.)
   Allegretto con moto.

(2) (*a*) Succession of two chords of the minor 9th of the first species, the first moving to the second by the descent of a minor 3rd, merely by change of root.

CLAUDE DEBUSSY.   *Children's Corner.*   (Durand, Pubr.)

(3) Chords of the 9th proceeding by minor thirds upwards.

CLAUDE DEBUSSY.   *Chansons de Bilitis.*   (Fromont, Pubr.)

(4) Successions of chords of the 9th of the 1st and 2nd species.

CLAUDE DEBUSSY.   *Chansons de Bilitis.*   (Fromont, Pubr.)

(5) Chords of the 9th proceeding by chromatic semitones.

CLAUDE DEBUSSY.   *Chansons de Bilitis.*   (Fromont, Pubr.)

(6) Common chords with appoggiaturas, or chords of the 9th with passing notes. Whichever interpretation be adopted, there is a succession of chords of the 9th proceeding by thirds upwards.

CLAUDE DEBUSSY. *Pelléas et Mélisande.* Page 233. (Durand, Pubr.)

(7) Chords of the 9th and the 7th alternately, by conjunct motion.
(*a*) 4th species.   (*b*) 2nd species.   (*c*) 4th species.

page 232.

(8) (*a*) Chords of the 9th proceeding by 3rds downwards.
     (*b*) Chords of the 9th proceeding by 3rds upwards.
     (*c*) Chords of the 9th proceeding by conjunct degrees.

page 80.

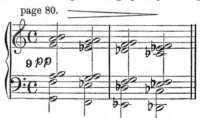

(9) Chords of the 9th by descending major seconds.

page 242.

(9)² Chords of the 9th by chromatic degrees.

FLORENT SCHMITT. *La Tragédie de Salomé.* (Jacques Durand, Pubr.)

Prélude. *Lento.*

(10) Inverted ninths (keys of B minor and A minor) on the unraised 7th degree, with dominant pedal.

FLORENT SCHMITT. *La Tragédie de Salomé.* (Jacques Durand, Pubr.)

Danse de l'Effroi.

(11) 4th inversion of the chord of the dominant 9th (key of G major).

FLORENT SCHMITT. *Psalm XLVI.* (Mathot, Pubr.)

(12) 9th with major 7th (that is, the chord of the 9th of the 4th species).

FLORENT SCHMITT. *Trois rapsodies.* (Durand, Pubr.)

(13) (*a*) Ninth with double alteration and anticipation in the upper part.

(14) (*a*) and (*b*) Chords of the 9th of which the root and the 9th appear at the interval of a 7th from one another by the 9th being below the root.

FLORENT SCHMITT. *Quintette pour piano et cordes.* (Mathot, Pubr.)

(15) (*a*) Dominant 9th complete, with, added, alterations of the 5th and the 7th.

(16) Resolution of the 9th.

CH. KŒCHLIN. *Le sommeil de Canope.* (Rouart & Lerolle.)

(17) (*a*) D♯ and G♯ appoggiaturas.

(*b*) 1st inversion of the chord of the dominant 9th, the root in the upper part and E an appoggiatura.

(*c*) D♯ an unresolved appoggiatura in chord of + ꝺ.

(*d*) Chord of + ꝺ, with E an unresolved appoggiatura.

(*e*) Chord of + ꝺ with F an appoggiatura.

(*f*) 2nd inversion of chord of the 9th.

(*g*) 2nd inversion of chord of the dominant minor 9th with B♮ appoggiatura.

(*h*) 2nd inversion of chord of the diminished 7th with G appoggiatura.

(*i*) Chord of the dominant minor 9th; A♯ is an appoggiatura and B♮ a passing pedal-note of the tonic. (Sustained from previous chord. Translator).

CH. KŒCHLIN.   *Chant de Kala Nag.*   (Rouart & Lerolle, Pubr.)

(18) Chords of the 9th proceeding by step at (*a*) and by diminished 4th at (*b*) with a note in common.   (F♯ = G♭.)

Study of Modern Harmony.

(19) (*a*) 3rd inversions of the chord of the major 9th proceeding by step (whole tone).

(*b*) 3rd inversions of the chord of the 9th, major and minor, proceeding by step (semitone).

(20) Succession, by descending semitone, of 3rd inversions of chord of the minor 9th.

CH. KŒCHLIN. *Prélude.*

(21) Succession of 1st inversions of chords of the 9th by conjunct degrees.

E. CHABRIER. *Le roi malgré lui* (1887). (Enoch, Pubr.)
page 339.

cresc.

E. CHABRIER. *Le roi malgré lui.* (Enoch, Pubr.)
page 229.

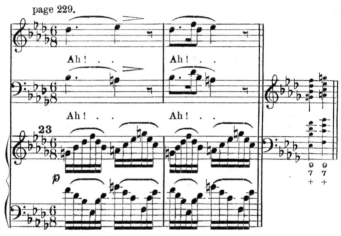

M. RAVEL. *Sur l'herbe.* (Durand, Pubr.)

(24) (*a*) The 9th against the root in the upper parts.   The root takes the character of a pedal in an inner part.

Although the foregoing explanation is
the better one, it may also be considered
that it is the G which forms the pedal.

M. RAVEL. *L'heure espagnole.*   (Durand, Pubr.)

(*a*) Pedal on F♯.
(*b*) Chords of the minor 9th with altered 5th proceeding by semitones.

etc.

(*c*) Pedal in inner part on F♮, taken and quitted regularly on an
integral note.   That makes a double pedal, F♯ — F♮.
(*d*) It is in the mind of the composer to consider the notation of the
song of the birds as a picturesque, extra-musical effect.   Particularly
is this so in that which concerns the first passage (Petit Coq), of which
the notation is only approximate.   This sound, which perhaps approxi-
mates to that of percussion instruments, is produced by the reed of the
double bassoon separated from the instrument.

M. RAVEL.   *Miroirs.*   (*Noctuelle*).   (Demets, Pubr.)

Très léger.

(26) Chords of the 9th by conjunct motion at (*a*), and by upward
3rd at (*b*), with appoggiatura and passing notes.

G. FAURE.   *Thême et Variations.*   (J. Hamelle, Pubr.)

Quasi adagio.

(27) Resolutions of chords of the 7th and of the 9th by 5th downwards.

Study of Modern Harmony.

Combination of chords of the major and minor 9th in progression by step.

(See Deductions No. 4).

Resolutions and successions of chords of the 9th (with or without alteration of the 5th).

Study of Modern Harmony.

C V   A V   F♯ V   D♯ V

Chord of the diminished 7th in four different forms, by changing the root. This combination belongs to the classical technique, as well as to modern harmony.

DEDUCTIONS

More than ever we must remember that the generalisations which follow are deductions founded upon the work of modern composers.

(1). (A). Two chords of the major 9th of the first species, in root position, may proceed by conjunct degrees (tone or semitone) ascending or descending, by similar motion in all the parts.*

Ascending: (4), (5), (22), (23).
Descending: (1), (8), (9), (18), (26).

The best arrangement
of the parts is that of      or,
the harmonics

(B). Two first inversions of chords of the major ninth of the first species proceed less easily under the same conditions. They are, nevertheless, (21) possible with careful disposition of the parts.

Second inversions, lending themselves to smooth arrangement of the parts, proceed easily.

Successions of third inversions under the same conditions of similar and conjunct motion, are practicable, though a little hard. (19).

---

* Notice this passage from the Finale of Franck's Symphony:

(2). (A). Two chords of the minor 9th of the first species in the root position, proceeding by conjunct degrees
and similar motion in all the parts, are not very agreeable,
when proceeding by whole tones. Nevertheless they may
be taken by semitone (25), particularly in descending.

(B). First inversions used under the same conditions are
disagreeable.

Successions of second and third inversions are not impracticable by semitone. (20).

The possibility of all these successions depends, as we have
said, *on the disposition of the parts.*

(3). In combining chords of the major ninth of the first
species with those of the minor ninth of the same species,
some interesting progressions are found, in the root position
as well as in the inversion. (19²), (28), (29).

(4). Chords of the major and minor ninth of the first
species proceed easily by major or minor thirds up or down.
(3), (6), (8), (31). Besides the progressions we have pointed
out, many others are possible by reason of the presence of
notes common to the two chords.

The same chord of the diminished 7th may be taken in
four different forms by changing the root. (32). This
combination belongs to the classical technique, but the
modern school draws from it new effects.

(5). The fourth inversion, which brings the ninth into the
bass (forbidden in classical technique), may readily be used.
(10), (11), Chap. XI (19).

In the inversions the root may be placed above the ninth,
at a distance of a seventh (14), (17) (a disposition taught by
Sabbatini at the end of the 18th century).

The ninth may approach the root at the distance of a
second * (24).

(6). With the new resolutions given to them by the
modern school, the chords of the 9th, by means of alterations,

---

* In the works of Bach, when the 8th is retarded by the 9th, this is
often found approached at the distance of a second.

FERDINAND KUFFERATH. *Ecole pratique du Choral.*

(Schott Brothers, Brussels.)

(13), (15), (25), (31); appoggiaturas (17), anticipations (13), etc., become valuable chords for harmonic research. We cannot too often repeat that the more or less agreeable sound of these progressions depends on the disposition of the parts, and also on the combination of tone qualities, if written for the orchestra.

Resolutions may be sought on all chords. (7), (16), (30.)

(7). Chords of the 9th of the second, third and fourth species are not, in actual fact, used very often (7), (12); they will be used, in the future, without doubt, like those of the first species.

CHAPTER IV

PREPARATION OF DISCORDS

At the present day all discords may be approached without preparation.* It matters not what modern work we may look at to be convinced of this.   We need give, therefore, but very few examples.**

SAMUEL ROUSSEAU.   *La Cloche du Rhin.*   (Choudens, Pubr.)
page 89.

(1) Chords of the $\frac{6}{4}$ moving a major second (or diminished 3rd) without either preparation or resolution.

page 32.

Chords of the $\frac{6}{4}$ by conjunct motion. The addition of a vocal part, nevertheless, allows of another interpretation. (See p. 32 of the Score.)

---

* For a long time there has been no question of the preparation of the minor 7th.

BEETHOVEN.   *Sonata Op. 31, No. 3.*

** On referring to Chapter X (Whole-Tone Scale) there will be found examples of the augmented fifth used freely.

V. D'INDY. *Lied Maritime.* (Rouart & Lerolle, Pubr.)

(3) $\frac{6}{4}$ chords without preparation.

CH. KŒCHLIN. *Extract from No. 4 (Epitaphe) of Etudes Antiques.*
(Suite Symphonique) (unpublished).

(4) (*a*) $\frac{6}{4}$ chords without preparation; notice also the fifths (*b*) and the false relation (*c*)).

CH. KŒCHLIN. *Le Vin.* (Rouart & Lerolle, Pubr.)

(5) Chord of the 7th of the 4th species without preparation.

DEBUSSY. *Pelléas et Mélisande.* Page 2. (Durand, Pubr.)
Très modéré.

(6) (*a*) Chords of the 7th without preparation.

THE SECOND

The whole modern school seems to be hypnotised by the interval of the second, which it writes at every turn.

Some discords which were taken successively as suspensions, as resolved appoggiaturas, and lastly as unresolved appoggiaturas, have given place to combinations of frequent use. In this combination of sounds the appoggiatura is heard at the same time as the principal note, which produces the interval of a second.

The two combinations most used are:

1. The sixth added to the Common Chord;—

This must not be confounded with the chord of ⁶₅. Here is the manner of its origin:

Suspension.　　Resolved　　Unresolved　Appoggiatura
　　　　Appoggiatura. Appoggiatura. sounded with
　　　　　　　　　　　　　　　the principal
　　　　　　　　　　　　　　　note.

2. The ninth added to the Common Chord;—

---

* We have already pointed out (page 9) this combination indicated by Père Sabbattini.

This is not a chord of the 9th, but is formed as follows:

Suspension.   Resolved   Unresolved   Appoggiatura
              Appoggiatura. Appoggiatura. sounded with
                                          the harmony
                                          note.

CLAUDE DEBUSSY. *Children's Corner*. (Durand, Pubr.)

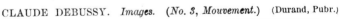

(a) Appoggiatura of a B♭ not heard.
(b) G♭, appoggiatura of F.
(c) Chord of B♭ with sixth added; —

CLAUDE DEBUSSY. *Images*. (*No. 3, Mouvement.*) (Durand, Pubr.)

(8) Succession of chords of +4 without 6ths, with passing notes.

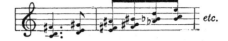 etc.

CLAUDE DEBUSSY. *Children's Corner.* (Durand, Pubr.)

(9) (*a*) F appoggiatura at same time as the principal note.

CLAUDE DEBUSSY. *Children's Corner.* (Durand, Pubr.)

'(10) Common Chord with sixth added.
(*b*) Appoggiatura without resolution (see Chapter VI).

CLAUDE DEBUSSY. *Children's Corner.* (Durand, Pubr.)

(11) 3rd inversion of chord of the 9th.

CLAUDE DEBUSSY. *Pelléas et Mélisande.* (Durand, Pubr.)

page 143.

Mais on m'a dit qu'ils ne s'aimaient pas

Modéré.

(12) Appoggiaturas without resolution   or otherwise.

M. RAVEL. *Miroirs (Alborada.)* (Demets, Pubr.)

Assez vif.

(13) (a) F♮ appoggiatura (on E♭) without resolution.
(b) C♮ appoggiatura (on B♭) without resolution.
(c) G♮ appoggiatura (on F♯) without resolution.

M. RAVEL *Miroirs (Alborada.)* (Demets, Publ.)

(14) (a) F♯, pedal in an inner part making the superimposed seconds:

M. RAVEL. *Miroirs (Noctuelles.)* (Demets, Publ.)

(15) (a) Change of position in the chord of the dominant 9th which may even result in 3 successive seconds.

(b) Appoggiatura of the 5th resolving very correctly on the following chord. Here is the passage written in 4 parts.

RENÉ LENORMAND. *Paysage pour les Veber's.* (Rouart & Lerolle, Pubr.)

(16) Chromatic scale at the major second, which can only be explained on the ground of its humorous intention.

SAMUEL ROUSSEAU. *La Cloche du Rhin.* Page 1. (Choudens, Pubr.)

(See Chap. V.)

ANDRÉ CAPLET. *Do, ré, mi, fa, sol.* (Monde Musical, Pubr.)

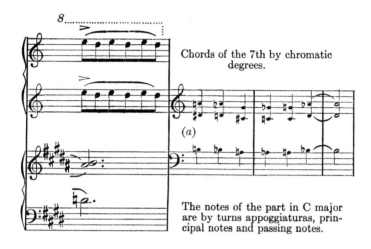

Chords of the 7th by chromatic
degrees.

The notes of the part in C major
are by turns appoggiaturas, principal notes and passing notes.

In his "Histoire de la Musique" (Vol. I, page 472), M.
Woollett quotes some curious examples from Rameau:

RAMEAU. *Platée.*

(*a*) Retardation of the F♯.
(*b*) Anticipation of the tonic.
(*c*) Appoggiatura against the
principal note.

(*a*) Ornamentation of the principal note and of a retardation of the
second.

CHAPTER V

NOTES FOREIGN TO THE CHORDS.
PASSING NOTES.   ORNAMENTS.

If fourths, fifths, sevenths, seconds, ninths may be written as harmony notes by similar and conjunct motion, one perceives that the modern school have allowed melody-notes to benefit by the same freedom.   It will be seen at the end of the chapter under what conditions they are now used.

SAMUEL ROUSSEAU. *La Cloche du Rhin.* (Choudens, Pubr.)

(1) (*a*) Truncated turn in the lower part.
(2) (*a*) Ornamentation of the major third.

SAMUEL ROUSSEAU. *La Cloche du Rhin.* (Choudens, Pubr.)

(3) Passing notes in augmented fourths and sixths.

SAMUEL ROUSSEAU. *La Cloche du Rhin.* (Choudens, Pubr.)

(*a*) Ornamentation with inner pedal on *B*.
(*b*) Ornamentation with inner and upper pedal on *B*.

page 1.   Explanation

(a) G♮ is a passing note.

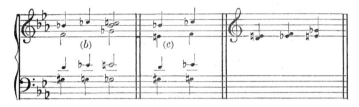

(b) C♭ E♭ G♮ passing notes.
(c) E♮ appoggiatura making its resolution simultaneously with the movement of the passing notes.

CH. KŒCHLIN. *Néère.* (Hachette, Pubr.)

(7) Ornamentation in fourths.

CH. KŒCHLIN. *Les Métaux.* (Rouart & Lerolle, Pubr.)

(8) (a) (b) Ornamentation by contrary motion (c) Ornaments making a chord of the 7th; nevertheless in the mind of the composer these combinations are written for their sonority without consideration of musical grammar.

CH. KŒCHLIN. *Berceuse phoque.*   (Rouart & Lerolle, Pubr.)

(9) Passing notes in chords of the second — a rapid succession of lightly played fourths for string quartet against sustained parts for voice and flute.

CH. KŒCHLIN. *Les Métaux.*   (Rouart & Lerolle, Pubr.)

(10) (*a*) F and A passing notes not preceded by the harmony note.

CH. KŒCHLIN. *Les Rêves morts.*   (Rouart & Lerolle, Pubr.)

(11) Passing notes in 7ths.

CH. KŒCHLIN.   *Berceuse phoque.*   (Rouart & Lerolle, Pubr.)

(12) Passing notes in fourths and in fifths by contrary motion. This is written with the effect of the orchestration in mind.

CH. KŒCHLIN.   *Berceuse phoque.*   (Rouart & Lerolle, Pubr.)

(13) (*a*) Passing notes in chords of the ninth.   Owing to the alteration of the 5th, the character of the chord of the 9th is annulled.   An
orchestral effect.

CH. KŒCHLIN.   *Accompagnement.*   (Rouart & Lerolle, Pubr.)

(14) Simultaneous ornaments by contrary motion.   (By Common
Chords.)

CH. KŒCHLIN. *Etudes symphoniques.* (unpublished.)

(15) (*a*) and (*b*) Ornamentation by Common Chords.

C. DEBUSSY. *Chansons de Bilitis.* (Fromont, Pubr.)

(16) (*a*) C♯ an auxiliary note (*b*) F× ornamentation below G♯
(*c*) E♯ ornamentation below F♯

ERNEST MORET. *Poème du silence.* (*Il pleut sur la mer.*)
(Heugel, Pubr.)

(17) Ornamentations at the 3rd and 5th by similar motion.

E. CHABRIER. *Gwendoline.* Page 94. (Enoch, Pubr.)

(18) Chords of $\frac{6}{4}$ consecutively, made by the ornaments in 4ths
(*a*) (*b*)

DÉODAT DE SÉVÉRAC.   *Le ciel est par dessus les toits.*

(*a*) Passing notes.

RENÉ LENORMAND.   *Paysage pour les Veber's.*

(Rouart & Lerolle, Pubr.)

(20) Passing notes in changing octaves.

Study of Modern Harmony.

(21)   (22)   Ornaments in augmented 4th and 6ths.

Study of Modern Harmony.

Ped.

(23) Ornaments in inverted 9ths.

M. RAVEL.   *Miroirs.*   (Durand, Pubr.)

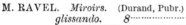

(24) Passing notes in 4ths.

SAINT-SAËNS.   *5th Concerto.*   (Durand, Pubr.)

(25) (*a*) Passing notes in fifths and sevenths. They have for their object the portrayal of an exuberance of joy, which is the character of the piece.

DEDUCTIONS

From the foregoing examples, it may be deduced that the Modern School employs passing notes and ornaments under the following conditions: —

Passing Notes

In seconds, in combination with appoggiaturas (6).
In minor thirds.   (Classical teaching.)
In major thirds.   Chap. X (6), (7).
In fourths (12), (24).
In fifths (12).
In augmented fifths.   Chap. X (1).
In sixths.   (Classical teaching.)
In sevenths (11), (25).
In thirds and sixths.   (Classical teaching.)
In fourths and sixths.   Chap. IV (4).
In augmented fourths and sixths (3).
In common chords (12).
In chords of the seventh (9), (13).
In chords of the ninth (13).
In changing octaves (20).
Without being preceded by the harmony note (10).

Ornaments

In seconds (16).
In minor thirds.   (Classical teaching.)
In major thirds (2), (4), (5).
In fourths (7).
In fifths (15), (17).   Chap. I (7), (17).
In sixths.   (Classical teaching.)
In thirds and sixths.   (Classical teaching.)
In fourths and sixths (18).   Chap. IV (4).
In augmented fourths and sixths (21), (22).
In common chords (14), (15), (17).
In chords of the seventh.   Chap. II (2).
In inverted chords of the ninth (23).

CHAPTER VI

APPOGGIATURAS

Chord-changing, either at the same moment as the resolution of an appoggiatura, or during the continuance of the
appoggiatura, is a procedure which may be found analysed
in treatises on Harmony. The suppression of the note of
resolution of the appoggiatura is a recent practice. This
artifice opens a perspective entirely new to lovers of the
unforeseen. One may thus write, by conjunct degrees, the
upper or lower auxiliary of any note whatever of a chord,
and then not trouble about it afterwards. . . But there
must be good reason for having recourse to this means; used
at all awkwardly it will easily give the impression of incoher-
ence. Good taste alone can serve as a guide.

MAURICE RAVEL. *Les grands vents venus d'outre mer.* (Durand, Pubr.)

(1) Appoggiaturas without resolutions. (See Chap. VIII, (4) where
the complete passage is analysed.)

M. RAVEL. *Sur l'herbe.* (Durand, Pubr.)

(2) Appoggiaturas without resolution.

M. RAVEL.   *Valses nobles et sentimentales.*   (Durand, Pubr.)

(3) This fragment is composed on a single chord

Let us now see the passage with the resolutions of the appoggiaturas, all of which resolutions take place only in bar *A*, where the chord changes its position:

The E (*a*) and (*b*) does not produce a change of chord. It is a passing note in both cases.

M. RAVEL. *MIROIRS* (*Oiseaux tristes*). (Demets, Pubr.)

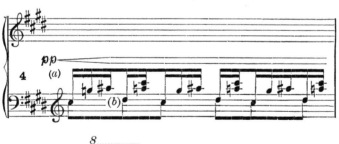

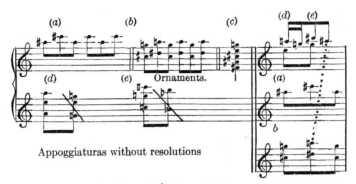

Appoggiaturas without resolutions

(*e*) In writing B♯ in place of C♯ the resolution on A♯ becomes quite natural, in spite of the presence of A♮ in the lower part, the ornamental character of which is evident.

CL. DEBUSSY.   *Chansons de Bilitis.*   (Fromont, Pubr.)

(*a*) E an appoggiatura making its resolution on D at the moment of the change of chord at (*c*)
(*b*) The same E (appoggiatura) becomes an integral note in the chord of the ninth.

(*a*) and (*c*) give

DÉODAT DE SÉVÉRAC.

(5²) See Chap. VIII (1), (2). Appoggiaturas without resolutions, or added ninth.

CH. KŒCHLIN.   *Les Rêves morts.*   (Rouart & Lerolle, Pubr.)

Moderato.

(*a*) G, appoggiatura without resolution.
(*b*) D♯ and F♯ appoggiaturas without resolutions.*
(*c*) G♮ appoggiatura without resolution.
(*d*) B, Tonic pedal.

---

* May be analysed classically. See the "Traité of Reber."

CH. KŒCHLIN. *L'astre rouge.* (Rouart & Lerolle, Pubr.)

(7) (*a*) G, Appoggiatura of F♯ without resolution. (*b*) E♭ Appoggiatura of D without resolution. (*c*) Chord of the 7th over the passing tonic.

CH. KŒCHLIN. *La sommeil de Canope.* (Rouart & Lerolle, Pubr.)

(*a*) C♯ Unresolved appoggiatura of B♭.
(*b*) A♮ Unresolved appoggiatura of G.
(*c*) B♮ Appoggiatura.
(*d*) B♭ Harmony note of + 2.
(*e*) Dominant minor ninth: the G♯ should be written A♭.
(*f*) Chord of the 9th.

WOOLLETT. *Intermezzo from Sonata for Piano and Violoncello.*
(Leduc & Bertrand, Pubrs.)

(*a*) G♭ Appoggiatura of F. (*b*) A♭ Appoggiatura of G♮.
(*c*) D♭ Appoggiatura of C. (*d*) E♭ Appoggiatura of D♮.

CH. KŒCHLIN.   *Le sommeil de Canope.*   (Rouart & Lerolle, Pubr.)

(a) Pedal; (b) F♯ passing note and ♭ $\frac{6}{7}$ of E on F♯ pedal;
(c) ♯$\frac{5}{4}$ on F♯. (d) E♮ Passing note; (e) D♯, E♯, G♯, B♮ appoggiatura-chord of the following chord, taken at the same time as the harmony notes in the lower 8ve.* (f) The same as the previous bar.

SAINT–SAËNS.   *Déjanire.*   (Durand, Pubr.)

(11) Appoggiaturas in chords of the diminished fifth. They represent the agonies of Hercules on wearing the fatal tunic.

---

*See foot-note on next page.

FLORENT-SCHMITT. *Psaume XLVI.* (Mathot, Pubr.)

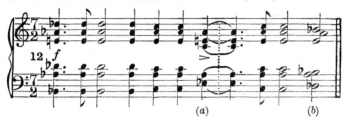

(12) (*a*) E♭ appoggiatura of the D♭ in the final chord (*b*).

---

* Foot-note to page 66.

MOZART. *L'Enlèvement au sérail.* (Translation Durdilly.) Page 74.

Mais   non   pas   d'un   fai - ble   cœur

The appoggiatura against the harmony note is of classical use:
(*a*) F♯ against G.   (*b*) E against F.   (*c*) C♯ against D.
It should be noticed that in the present case the tone-qualities are different.
In quotation (10) the harmony notes are at the octave below.

BEETHOVEN. *Finale of the 9th Symphony.*

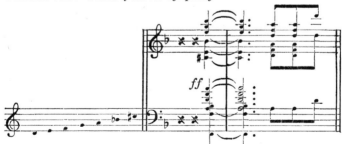

Here is a characteristic example from Beethoven, in which the chord of the 7th on C♯ as appoggiatura to the chord of D minor is attacked at the same time as the latter, so that all the notes of the scale of D minor are heard together.

ALBERT ROUSSEL. *Bourrée.* (Rouart & Lerolle, Pubr.)

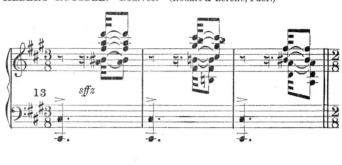

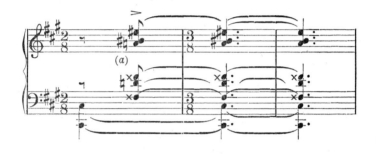

(13) Somewhat complicated as they are in appearance these harmonies
(*a*) (*b*) (*c*) are composed of appoggiatures of the chord of C♯ major (*d*).

DEDUCTIONS

1. **The** foregoing quotations bear specially on the unresolved appoggiatura. As we have said, the use of this
artifice depends only upon the good taste of the individual;
only musicians in whom is an artistic intuition strong enough
to take the place of the rule should use it. (1), (2), (3),
(4), (6), (7), (8).
Chap. III (17); Chap. IV (7), (13).

2. It is evident that from the moment that it became
possible to make progressions of all kinds of harmonic
combinations by step and by similar motion of all the parts,
the modern school found itself authorised to treat appoggiaturas simultaneously by similar movement under the same
conditions of freedom.

It may be observed that if a chord is of the character of
an "appoggiatura" as regards all its notes, and if it moves
by similar motion, there results a succession of two identical
chords. The first preserves the character of an appoggiatura only by the nature of the neighbouring harmonies, or
by the presence of a pedal.

CHAPTER VII

ANCIENT DEVICES (*) { Imitations
{ Sequences
BAR-LINES
FALSE RELATIONS.   PEDALS
MELODIC INTERVALS

Imitations.

This artifice of traditional writing tends to disappear. Certain composers have completely renounced its use; others, and they, perhaps, form the greatest number, use it only to enhance the piquancy of the harmonic colouring.   Musicians of a classical education continue to utilise it with all the simplicity of a school exercise.   It would be as wrong to proscribe it entirely as to abuse it.   All that can contribute to the realisation of the artistic ideal conceived by the composer it is good to use. (1), (2), (3).

Sequences.

For long, in technical studies, an excessive use was made of sequences, a matter which can only be regarded as deplorable, for it inculcates in the pupil a taste for easy formulas.   The Sequence is the mother of the "Rosalia." The examples which one meets with seem to have been inspired by a recollection of the school, rather than by any æsthetic idea (7).   Nevertheless, in certain cases they may correspond with a dramatic sentiment or assist the expansion of the melodic outline.

---

* There need be no question here of the combinations, scarcely to be called musical, which entertained the masters of the XVth century. Very happily, works conceived in this spirit are to be met with only rarely in the modern period: —

B. DAMCKE. — PRELUDE in 4 parts for organ or piano in counterpoint by retrograde and contrary motion.   (Richaut, Pubr., about 1865.)

RENÉ LENORMAND. — DIVERTISSEMENT AMÉRICAIN for piano duet in counterpoint by retrograde and contrary motion. (J. Hamelle, Pubr., c. 1875.)

With no artistic interest this kind of music can be considered only as a virtuosity of technique in writing.

Bar-Lines.

It does not seem to us paradoxical to say that among the obstacles raised by the theorists against the development of musical thought, the most serious is that of the bar-line. It was at the outset — towards the end of the 16th century — a means of facilitating execution, and in the character of " *guide âne*," a finger post,* it rendered and still renders great services which make it difficult for us to dispense with it. But its action is not limited to these services. Little by little the notes have grouped themselves otherwise than in this bar, taking in the mind of the composer an importance relative to their position; that which precedes the bar is feebly accented, that which follows immediately is struck strongly — weak beat, strong beat. The mind of the great musicians is itself warped by the power of that habit.** The classical theorists have imposed on them the division by four measures: "The Carrure."

Without having any pedagogic intention, we counsel all young musicians to habituate themselves to think and to write without taking any account of the question of bar-lines. After that, to facilitate reading, they will add bar-lines before the accented parts of their musical discourse. From that will proceed measures of all sorts; but what does this matter?***

(See "L'Abbaye" of Koechlin, where measures of $\frac{6}{4}$ $\frac{7}{4}$ $\frac{4}{2}$ $\frac{3}{2}$ alternate, and also "Rhodante," of the same author, where are found measures of $\frac{6}{8}$ $\frac{9}{4}$ $\frac{3}{2}$ $\frac{3}{4}$ $\frac{5}{4}$ $\frac{7}{8}$ **** (8), (17).)

False Relations.

What is to be said of the false relation of the tritone? Reber found the rules "obscure and contradictory." They are now no more; no one bothers much about the false relation of the tritone. It was inadmissible that the two notes of a harmonic interval on which rested the actual tonality should be heard in two neighbouring chords. Two major thirds in succession by whole tones were forbidden,

---

* "A help to feeble minds and bad counters." Morley (Tr.).

** We may point here to the remarkable studies on Rhythm and Time of M. Jean d'Udine. We believe he is not far from sharing our point of view. In any case, his new and very personal views are of the very highest interest for musicians.

*** M. H. Woollett in his "Pièces d'étude" (Leduc & Bertrand, Pub.), gives a general list of all the bar-measures, which are to the number of fifty.

**** The Andante and Finale of the 2nd Symphony of Borodine, comprise continual changes of time.

because they produced the false relation of the tritone; **for**
a long time major thirds *have* been so written, so we need
say no more.   (See Chapter X.)

The question of the false relation of the octave is more
delicate;   nevertheless the best authors write it, but so
skilfully as to draw from it happy effects. (4), (5), (6), (9).

Pedals.*

The solid pedals of the tonic and dominant on which all
the masters have piled up vivid progressions, preparations
for the great climax, ingenious "stretti," etc., have not failed
to come under the influence of modern times (13), (15), (16).
A melodic outline may be taken as a pedal (10), (11); in
other cases the pedal is so short that it may be called a
"passing pedal" (12). If, in their origin (10th century),
pedals were a naïve procedure for sustaining the voice,** they
have become, in modern writing, a source of harmonic
complexity.

(*)

GOUNOD.   *Ulysse.*   (Choudens, Pubr.)

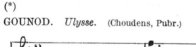

Se   so - leil monte   et brû - le

This is bold harmony for the period at which it was written. We
recall, to the honour of the celebrated composer, that he interested
himself in musical evolution, and more than one young composer found
in him a warm defender.

** Primitively the hurdy-gurdy (vielle), and the bagpipes (corne-
muse) were intended to make the tonic heard in the bass, in a continu-
ous manner;   it is known that the Arabs accompanied their heroic
songs with a sustained note on the Rebec.

EXAMPLES

G. FAURÉ. *La bonne Chanson.* (*Op. 61, No. 6.*) (J. Hamelle, Pubr.)

Allegro moderato.

(1) Imitation.

(2) Imitation.

G. FAURÉ. *La Fée aux Chansons.* (J. Hamelle, Pubr.)

Allegretto vivo (molto meno mosso)

(3) Imitation.

G. FAURÉ.   *Le Parfum impérissable.*   (J. Hamelle, Pubr.)

(4) False relation.

G. FAURÉ.   *Les Présents.*   (J. Hamelle, Pubr.)

(5) False relation.

M. RAVEL.   *Miroirs.*   (*Oiseaux tristes.*)   (Durand, Pubr.)

The G♮ being an appoggiatura, according to classical technique there is no false relation. The same remark applies to the other chords.

S. ROUSSEAU.   *La Cloche du Rhin.*   (Choudens, Pubr.)

Allegro moderato.   page 118

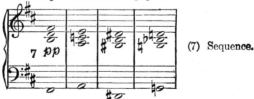

(7) Sequence.

M. RAVEL. *Sainte.* (Durand, Pubr.)

(8)   Bar of one beat.

S. ROUSSEAU. *La Cloche du Rhin.*   Page 31.   (Choudens, Pubr.)

(9)   (*a*) Chromatic false relation.

CH. KŒCHLIN. *Le Vaisseau.* (Rouart & Lerolle, Pubr.)
Voice & Orchestra.

(The figure which serves as a pedal is prepared in the previous bars.)

more and more

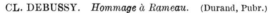

Musical and expressive effect: drifting of the vessel, distress, solitude and bitterness.

CL. DEBUSSY.   *Hommage à Rameau.*   (Durand, Pubr.)

(11) (*a*) Melodic outline forming two inverted pedals a third apart.
(*b*) Pedal in the bass.

CH. KŒCHLIN. *Soir Païen.* (Rouart & Lerolle, Pubr.)

(a) F♯ root of a chord of the 9th; (b) F♯ appoggiatura of E; A♮ appoggiatura of G; (c) B transient tonic pedal; (d) Pedals, B♭ and F.

GABRIEL DUPONT. *La maison dans les dunes.* (Heugel, Pubr.)

(13)   (*a*) A note foreign to the harmony forming an inner pedal.

GABRIEL DUPONT. *La Glu.* (ACT IV.) (Heugel, Pubr.)

Pedal in the bass on which are imposed remote harmonies. After taking knowledge of the foregoing chapters, the reader can explain all the successions of chords by means of alterations and appoggiaturas.

M. RAVEL. *Gaspard de la nuit.* (*Le gibet*). (Durand, Pubr.)

A particularly interesting example of an inner pedal. The whole piece might be quoted, as that note, sometimes A♯, sometimes B♭, is not abandoned for a single instant, in the midst of the most disturbing harmonies, complicated by unresolved appoggiaturas.

PAUL DUKAS. *Ariane et Barbe Bleue.* Page 97. (Durand, Pubr.)

(a) One of the upper parts approaches the pedal F♯ from the distance of a semitone. There will be found a number of interesting examples of pedals in this score.

CH. KŒCHLIN.   *Etudes antiques No 1.*   (*Suite Symphonique.*)

(Unpublished.)

Example of changes of bars, (or rather, of phrases), written origi-
nally without bar-lines.

Melodic Intervals.

All treatises on harmony devote a chapter to the melodic
intervals permitted or forbidden.

Nevertheless, the Breton labourer, the boatman on the
Volga, the camel driver of the desert — to whom Nature has
suggested admirable songs, as though to deride professional
musicians — none of these anonymous composers have consulted treatises of harmony to know what they have the
right to sing and often they have used melodic intervals
said to be forbidden.

That there are some intervals more or less easy to attack
is incontestable, but a "musician" will write no melodies
except those possible to sing, if he writes for the voice; and
instruments do not recognize difficulties of intonation.

The question may, therefore, be looked at under two
aspects:

1. In writing for instruments all intervals are accessible;
2. In writing for the voice the freedom of writing is limited only by greater or less facility of execution.

Large bodies of voices deprived of accompaniment succeed
ill in enharmonic progressions.

Voices doubled by an accompaniment can approach all
intervals. Voices without accompaniment, or with an
accompaniment that does not double the voice parts, hesitate
in approaching certain intervals.

For example, the following intervals are difficult to sing:

We may conclude that the voice is opposed to the subtleties of our system, because the same sounds (tempered) become easy to approach by changing the notation.

The composer might do well to sing all he has written for the voice, when he would be able to judge if it were possible. . . . . But there are no *forbidden* melodic intervals.

---

* The partisans of the division of the octave into twelve equal semitones do not fail to tell us that if their system were adopted these complications of Notation would no longer exist. "Nature does not know the derivative notes, and each number of vibrations produces a fundamental and unique sound, and must consequently have its own name and not be tributary to the note which precedes, or to that which follows." *Système Musical Menchaca.*

CHAPTER VIII

TO END A PIECE

The ear is so accustomed to the perfect cadence or the plagal cadence as the termination of all polyphonic compositions, that most hearers do not consider a piece finished which has not the chord of the tonic as its final chord.

Nevertheless, this commonplace close may be found to be in contradiction to what has gone before. To quote an example in a well-known piece: —

Everybody knows the admirable "Erlking" of Schubert, in which the author has shown so dramatic and poignant a sentiment. At the close of the song — where the father perceives that he has in his arms only the dead body of his son — Schubert, submitting to inexorable custom, (he must definitely finish), concludes with the most commonplace of perfect cadences.

Schumann, who was a great innovater — a fact too often forgotten — knew how to rid himself of this restraint in "The Soldier." A poor devil, in order to show himself a good soldier, carried out the order to shoot his best friend; his despair troubled Schumann, who, as a true philosopher, sees rising before him a problem of the psychology of duty; he pauses immediately, modifies the character of his harmonies and finishes on the dominant, with no tonic conclusion, making the hearer a sharer in the sentiments which animate him. The modern school has followed him in this path, and the character of that which has gone before prompts the special kind of termination to be adopted.

Here are some examples of terminations other than those made by perfect or plagal cadences.*

---

* GOUNOD. *Sapho.* Page 191. (Choudens, Pubr.)

BOURGAULT–DUCOUDRAY closes the "Rapsodie Cambodgienne" (Heugel, Publisher) on a chord of the 7.

DÉODAT DE SÉVÉRAC. *Le ciel est par dessus le toit.*

(Edition mutuelle.)

A finish with the 9th added to the chord of the tonic.

DÉODAT DE SÉVÉRAC. *Un rêve.* (Edition mutuelle.)

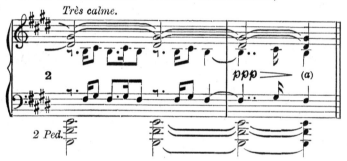

The D♯ and F♯ may be considered as appoggiaturas of E without resolution.

RENÉ LENORMAND. *Pièces exotiques.* (J. Hamelle, Pubr.)

A close with the 6th added to the chord of the tonic.

M. RAVEL.   *Les grands vents venus d'outre mer.*   (Durand, Pubr.)

(*a*) Appoggiatura without resolution.   Interesting as a termination, this passage calls on other grounds for a careful examination.

For greater clearness, here is the harmonic progression denuded of its passing notes and appoggiaturas (in D♯ minor for simplicity).

Appoggiatura ascending and descending from the D♯ without resolution.

CH. KŒCHLIN. *L'Eau.* (Rouart & Lerolle, Pubr.)

Sixths and ninths added to the common chord, or, appoggiaturas without resolutions.

FLORENT SCHMITT.   *Glas.*   (Mathot, Pubr.)

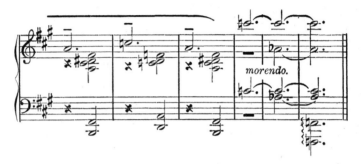

An unexpected close of great effect on the chord of F minor.

E. CHABRIER.   *Le roi malgré lui.*   (Enoch, Pubr.)

CHAPTER IX

SCALES — TONALITY

"The diatonic major scale may, therefore, be considered, if de-sired, as a rational product of the resonance of sonorous bodies, and having as its origin a single sound which is the base of the system; but on condition that it is regarded as a "manufactured product," of which human genius has determined the definite form according to its tastes and aptitudes."

LAVIGNAC.*
(*La Musique et les Musiciens, Delagrave.*)

"Scales do not exist; tonality alone exists and two modalities; the rest is free from all constraint."

J. HURÉ.
(*Dogmes Musicaux.*)**

"The scale does not exist. It is a formula of convention."

DERODE.
(*Introduction a l'étude de l'harmonie, Paris, 1828.*)

It is impossible to quote here all the musical scales em-ployed from the most ancient times. We will confine ourselves to pointing out those which can be utilized by the modern school, or which present some interest on the ground of curiosity.

In his "Traité d'harmonie" (Lemoine, Publisher), Gevaert gives an excellent study of the diatonic pentaphone, or penta-tonic scale. (I have adopted the French word here as being more convenient than the rather unweildy term "pentatonic scale,") which he considers to be older than the Greek sys-tem, and which is still to be met with among the Mongols, the Chinese, the Japanese, the aborigenes of America and the Celts of the British Isles.***

---

* Among all the musicians who have expressed this opinion, we have selected a professor of the Conservatoire of Paris (M. Lavignac), a composer known for his enlightened liberalism (M. Jean Huré), and a theorist of 1830 (M. Derode).

** *Monde Musical* of July 30th, 1911.

*** Several of Wagner's themes are based on the diatonic pentaphone.

R. WAGNER. *Rheingold.* (Schott, London and Mayence, and Eschig, Paris.)

The following are different modes of the diatonic penta-phone:

These four modes may commence and finish on the dominant. It will be noticed that the scales comprise no semitones.

* * *

M. Woollett in his "Histoire de la Musique," (Monde Musical and Joseph Williams, Limited), gives us a mass of curious information concerning the ancient Hindoo scales (Volume I, page 40). It is impossible for us to write down these scales, because, except for the fifth degree, which corresponds exactly to our true fifth, all the other degrees are raised or lowered by a "srouti," an interval a little larger than a quarter tone. Some treatises of music in the Sanscrit language, dating 2,000 years before the Christian Era, disclose this system, in which the octave comprises 22 "sroutis."

* * *

If we examine the music of the Greeks, we must fix precisely the period of which we wish to speak; Greek antiquity comprises about twelve centuries during which music was continually being transformed. In the time of the Pelasgians, the scale of ¼ tones, that which constitutes the kind known as "enharmonic," was used:

¼ tone – ¼ tone – major 3rd – 1 tone – ¼ tone – ¼ tone – major 3rd.

Octave *

---

* Fétis. Preface to the 7th edition of his "Traité d'harmonie." In spite of the vast erudition of the celebrated Belgian musicographer, his assertions have been several times contested: we leave him responsible for this scale.

Later, the Hellenes, after having conquered Peloponnesus, substituted the ⅓ of the tone for the ¼ tone.

But if the oriental chromaticism spread in Greece in consequence of successive invasions, some peoples, the Dorian among others, remained hostile to the subdivision of the tone. The most ancient Greek mode that is known is the Dorian mode:

to which may be added the Phrygian mode:

and the Lydian mode:

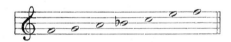

These scales were modified and completed little by little; other modes sprang up; chromaticism and enharmonicism manifested themselves in each of these modes, only to be abandoned later; at last, in the time of Aristoxenus, the musical system of the Greeks, of a learned complexity, included 13 modes; a little later the number was increased to 15 modes, but six of these were merely transpositions*.

Leaving on one side these six transposed scales, and bringing the nine others to a uniform starting point, we have the following:**

---

* We cannot speak of Greek music without quoting the admirable studies of F. A. Gevaert: "Histoire de la Musique dans l'antiquité, Les Problèmes musicaux d'Aristotle, la Mélopée antique dans le chant de L'Eglise latine; Histoire er Théorie de la Musique grecque; Traité d'harmonie, 1st Part (Lemoine, Publisher).

** We borrow this table from the "Traité de Contrepoint" of Richter (Breitkopf & Hartel, Publishers, Leipsic).

1. Hypo-dorian or Aeolian.

2. Hypo-phrygian.

3. Hypo-lydian.

4. Dorian.

5. Phrygian.

6. Lydian.

7. Hyper-dorian or Mixo-lydian.

8. Hyper-Phrygian or Locrian.

9. Hyper-lydian.

* The sign + indicates a note added to complete the octave when the two tetrachords overlap. If the added note is at the bottom of the scale the prefix Hypo is joined to the name of the mode; if it is at the top of the scale the prefix Hyper is used.

The following are the eight Ecclesiastical tones instituted by Saint Ambrose and Saint Gregory:

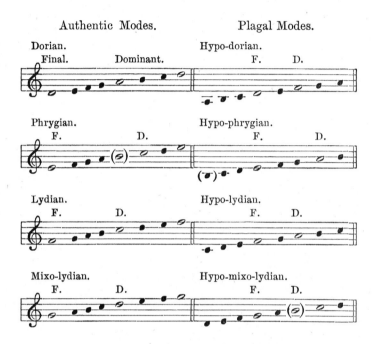

Authentic Modes.   Plagal Modes.

Dorian.   Hypo-dorian.

Phrygian.   Hypo-phrygian.

Lydian.   Hypo-lydian.

Mixo-lydian.   Hypo-mixo-lydian.

Later, six new modes were added, but two among them were found to be anti-melodic, so that four only were retained, which brought up to twelve the number of the Church tones, authentic and plagal.

Aeolian.   Hypo-aeolian.

Ionian.   Hypo-ionian.

Until the 10th or 11th century these modes were called 1st mode, 2nd mode, etc. Since that time the earlier Greek denominations were again used, but these have not always been applied to the corresponding mode, an important point for those who wish to make researches in the music of that period.

The many scales we have enumerated offer to the composer certain resources which can be utilised in modern polyphony.

* * *

After giving up the bizarre and monstrous hexachordal system* musicians came little by little to use only one series, the major scale: —

From this scale the minor scale, which appears in three aspects, was drawn. (We leave on one side the questions of the origins of the major and minor scales.)

Composers continually mingle these three forms.

---

* For a long period the paternity of this system was quite wrongly attributed to Guido d'Arezzo. In his "Micrologue" he says explicitly: "There are 7 notes and we cannot have more than seven; just as after the seven days of the week the same days repeat themselves in the same manner as before, and the first and the eighth bear the same name, so the first and the eighth notes must be represented by the same sign, because we feel that they produce the same sound." ("Histoire de la Musique moderne," Marcillac).

A very clear exposition of the hexachordal system will be found in "La Musique et les Musiciens" of Lavignac. Page 461, (Delagrave, Publisher).

By raising or lowering the notes of the diatonic scale we obtain the chromatic scale which may be presented under different aspects due to the notation employed.

(i) All the notes may be raised with the exception of the 6th degree which passes to the 7th by lowering this latter note:

(This scale corresponds to the major chromatic mode.)

(ii) All the notes may be lowered with the exception of the 4th degree, which passes to the 5th by an upward alteration; —

(This scale corresponds to the minor chromatic mode.)

(iii) All the notes may be lowered; —

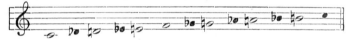

or, (iv) all the notes may be raised; —

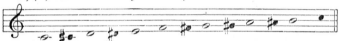

or, (v) again, a mixture of raised and lowered notes is found; —

(a)

(b)

The chromatic scale (really imaginary since it is impracticable on all instruments with fixed notes) is therefore:

that is to say, seventeen sounds represented by twelve.

To these scales may be added many others:*

That of Hauptmann:—

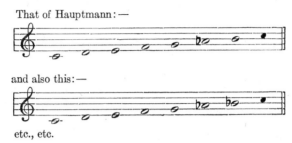

and also this:—

etc., etc.

M. Busoni, in a study on musical scales, (Breitkopf & Hartel) describes one hundred of them.

* * *

Whilst the Western races eliminated the small variable intervals, the Oriental races remained faithful to scales of one-third and one-quarter tones. The transcription of these scales is impossible by means of modern European notation — except for some which approximate to our system, but which it is necessary to say that the Orientals declare to be false when we execute them. The use of the interval of the augmented second, by which we think to give an Oriental impression, is for them a coarse proceeding, which wounds the extreme delicacy of their auditory organ.

M. Bourgault-Ducoudray in his "Mélodies populaires de la Grèce et de l'Orient," gives us an Oriental chromatic scale.

Commencing on the dominant.   Commencing on the tonic.

M. Woollett in his "Pièces d'Etudes,"** gives a table of various tonalities, from which we take the following Oriental scale:

---

* M. Anselme Vinée, in his work "Principes du Système musical et de l'Harmonie" (J. Hamelle, Publisher), brings forward an interesting study on altered scales.

** Leduc & Bertrand, Publishers.

He gives besides some examples of scales which may be formed by oneself by the mixing of tetrachords or the alteration of certain degrees.

The modern Greek Church still possesses the oriental chromaticism.

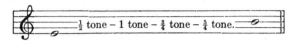
$\frac{1}{2}$ tone – 1 tone – $\frac{3}{4}$ tone – $\frac{5}{4}$ tone.

Pére Thibaut in a very interesting study* shows a comparative table of the Turkish scale — a division of the octave into 23 intervals — and the Syrian scale of Meshaqa — a division of the octave into 25 intervals.**

* * *

Modern authors make use of a scale of whole tones, which gives a succession of six notes without a leading note:

see Chap. X.

This is an important fact, because the resulting harmonic combinations destroy the shape and character of the tonality which, by comparison with the Greek tonalities, is called modern.

We have already drawn attention to the scale of M. Menchaca, consisting of equal semitones and giving a scale of twelve degrees.

M. Scriabine makes use of a scale formed from the harmonics 8 to 14, but omitting the 12th:

As a pleasantry, futurist musicians claim the use of the "commatic" scale, that is, the division of the octave into fifty-three commas. We may, without being taxed with naïveté, take this demand into consideration, because the

---

* See "La Revue Musicale S. I. M." of 15th February, 1910.

** There may be read in the "Historie de la Musique" of Woollett (Volume I) the study of the Syriac scales (Jacobite or Syrian rite) after Dom Parisot; there will be found also an interesting review of keys and modes used in the Maronite, Coptic, Abyssinian, Ethiopian and Armenian Churches.

division of the octave into small intervals is in use in the modern East. It is not a new idea; 2,000 years before Christ (see page 88), the Hindoos, futurists without knowing it, divided the octave into twenty-two "srouties." Besides, there exists in the Imperial Museum at St. Petersburg, an organ or harmonium, in which the octave is divided into fifty-three intervals; the keys are of different colours and arranged on five keyboards.

In principle we see no objection to the making of scales of small intervals, each race being free to choose the succession of sounds which best meets the expression of its sentiments. But beyond a certain limit the auditory organ can catch nothing but a confused noise.

*   *   *

It may be useful to recall that by tonality is meant the complete relationship established between the different elements of a series of sounds, those relationships grouping themselves around the first note of the series, the tonic.

The modern school modulates continually and with the greatest skill; the most remote tonalities are approached with facility by ingenious successions, and the change of mode which brings together more remote tonalities is always ready to come in. Besides, as the chord of the dominant seventh characterises a key, from the moment when several can be used in succession that which is called modulation — that is to say, the preparation of a new tonality — is found to be very much modified. It is no longer a group of chords that prepares a new key, it is a series of progressions of passing keys, of which the whole determines the feeling of a principal tonality.

Everybody knows that the distance from one key to another key depends upon the number of sharps and flats which differentiates them, but it must be noticed that when there are more than six sharps or flats between the two scales, they have no longer any notes in common.

In the classical style, it was considered that the keys formed upon the degrees of the diatonic scale (II, III, IV, V and VI) constituted the series of possible modulations from the principal key; the substitution of minor for major, and *vice versâ* further increased the number of these dependent keys. Now, one modulates to each degree of the chromatic scale and regards it as the tonic. Whether the composer limits himself to exploring the neighbouring keys, or whether he approaches the remote keys, he must never forget that a well-considered passage draws its value, its effect, from that which precedes and that which follows. He must never sacrifice the line of logical succession of keys and chords to the pleasure of writing a curious harmonic example.

CHAPTER X

ON THE WHOLE-TONE SCALE

This combination of notes is often used by the **modern** school, who draw from it curious successions of chords of the augmented fifth.*

The whole-tone scale has only six notes, and has no leading-note. It cannot terminate on the octave except by having recourse to the enharmonic.

Since it finds its inspiration in the old division of the scale into tetrachords, the whole tone scale can be divided into two tetrachords, the last note of the first being the first note of the second, which fixes the position (the 4th degree) of the enharmonic change.

---

* Wagner used chords of the augmented fifth, but most **frequently** by chromatic degrees, which gives them a different character from the examples quoted on **pages 101** and following.

WAGNER. *Tristan und Isolde.*   (Breitkopf & Hartel.)

(*a*) By chromatic degrees.

In harmonising this scale we have a chord of the augmented fifth on each degree:

In consequence of the identity of sound of the augmented fifth and the minor sixth these chords are reduced to two:

The scale in thirds will be as follows:

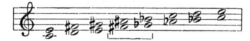

and by contrary motion:

---

* WAGNER.   *Siegfried.*   (Schott, London and Mayence, and Eschig, Paris.)

(*b*) By minor thirds in the bass.

We may also have the scale in chords by contrary motion:

It will be noticed that the notes of each chord of the descending scale are the same in sound as the notes of the corresponding chord of the ascending scale.

For those who are not afraid of the harshness of the discords* we may point to a curious arrangement of the scale of whole tones. In each chord the six notes of the scale are heard.

---

* The basis of the harmony of M. Scriabine's "Prometheus," is the following chord, which he treats as a perfect concord. (Nicolas Petroff. *Monde Musical* 1911) (see also Clutsam, *Musical Times* 1913. H.A.)

We are a long way from the time when the third was treated as a dissonance; besides, the classing of intervals as consonances and dis-consonances is arbitrary. It may be said that, theoretically, there is but one consonance, the unison, of which the relation is represented by $\frac{1}{1}$; the farther removed from this simple relation, the less is the interval consonant, but the point where "dissonance" begins must vary according to the susceptibilities of the ear.

These combinations are not much used in the form of scales by contrary motion (11), but, taking them by themselves, one may seek and find some entertaining progressions, because each of these combinations is identical in sound with a chord of the ninth of which the fifth is doubled and altered, ascending or descending (8);

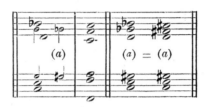

The same interpretation obtains with the other combinations.

In these scales we have indicated the enharmonic change. In practice the diminished third is approached openly:

DEBUSSY. **2**

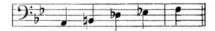

and in the scales of thirds the skip of the diminished third is made successively in the two parts, which brings about two diminished fourths in succession. See Debussy (6) and Saint-Saëns (7).

Lastly, the enharmonic character of these six chords which reduce themselves to two makes it possible to use alternatively the forms ♯5, ⁶₃ and ⁶₄; Debussy (6).

There exists a second scale of whole tones; that which has for its point of departure: C♯.

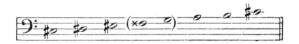

All that we have said with regard to the former scale may be applied to the latter.

There are no other whole-tone scales. Every other point of departure than C or C♯, brings about only a reproduction of these two scales.

CH. KŒCHLIN.   *L'Astre rouge.*   (Rouart & Lerollé), Pubr.)

Et le rou - ge Sa - hil   du fond des

nuits   tra - gi - ques   seul   fiam - be et

Explanation.

The whole on a pedal A.

CL. DEBUSSY. *Children's Corner.* (Durand, Pubr.)

CL. DEBUSSY. *Prélude (piano).* (Fromont, Pubr.)

A. BRUNEAU. *Le Rêve.* (1891). (Choudens, Pubr.)

CL. DEBUSSY. *Prélude.* (Fromont, Pubr.)

Whole-tone scale with interval of the diminished third.

CL. DEBUSSY. *Pelléas et Mélisande.* Page 236. (Durand, Pubr.)

(*a*) One part makes a skip of a diminished third, the other continuing by whole tones, which gives two diminished fourths to the point where the second part in its turn makes a skip of a diminished third (*b*).

SAINT-SAËNS. *Scherzo.* Op. 87, page 2. (Durand, Pubr.)

Another example of the same progressions.

H. WOOLLETT. *Sonata in F♯ minor.* (Leduc & Bertrand, Pubr.)
(*Piano and Violoncello.*)

An example of all the notes of the whole tone scale being heard simultaneously. (*a*) Chord of the dominant ninth on B (in E major)

with ascending alteration of the fifth F♯ (written G for F✕), and descending alteration of the same fifth F♯ (written E♯ for F♮). The ninth, C♯, approaches the root at a distance of a second which gives:

CL. DEBUSSY. *Pelléas et Mélisande.*   Page 111.   (Durand, Pubr.)

CL. DEBUSSY. *Pelléas et Mélisande.*   Page 4.   (Durand, Pubr.)

CH. KŒCHLIN. *La Guerre.*   (Rouart & Lerolle, Pubr.)

Chords of the augmented fifth by contrary motion, causing all the notes of the whole tone scale to be heard simultaneously.

CHAPTER XI

VARIOUS HARMONIES

FLORENT SCHMITT.   *Tristesse au jardin.*   (Mathot, Pubr.)

Augmented eleventh.   This is the harmonic eleventh added to the ninth.

CL. DEBUSSY.   *Chansons de Bilitis.*   (Fromont, Pubr.)

(*a*) D♯ appoggiatura and afterwards ornamentation of C♯.
(*b*) A♯ and C♯ melodic
figure forming a pedal.

A♯ being equisonant with
B♭ we may also say:

CL. DEBUSSY.   *Chansons de Bilitis.*   (Fromont, Pubr.)

The transposition of the chord (*a*) readily explains this passage.
(*b*) is a second inversion of the chord of the 9th on the dominant E♭;
or a chord of the ninth, A♭ and C being appoggiaturas of G and B♭; or
still further a chord of the 11th on B♭.   (*c*) Passing notes going through
the chord.

CL. DEBUSSY.   *Chansons de Bilitis.*   (Fromont, Pubr.)

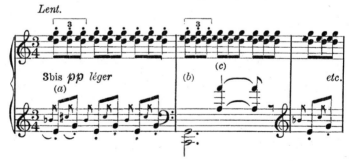

Chords are written for their sonority; it is therefore not necessary that they should all be fully explained. In the present case, the effect of the A (*c*) is so mysteriously poetic and so adequate to the sense of the words which precede that one would hardly think of asking from whence it is derived.

Nevertheless it may be said:

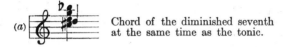

(*a*)   Chord of the diminished seventh at the same time as the tonic.

(*b*) D retardation of C.
(*c*) A, unresolved appoggiatura, or added sixth.

It may be interesting to analyse A as a passing note in changing octaves.

CLAUDE DEBUSSY. *Children's Corner.* (Durand, Pubr.)

Tonic and dominant pedal, with melody accompanied by the fourth below. See Chap. I, page 12, Note on Organum.

CLAUDE DEBUSSY. *Hommage à Rameau.* (Durand, Pubr.)

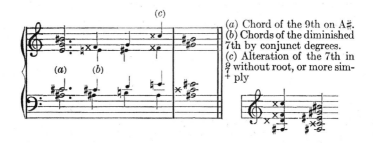

(*a*) Chord of the 9th on A♯.
(*b*) Chords of the diminished 7th by conjunct degrees.
(*c*) Alteration of the 7th in $^9_7$ without root, or more simply

CLAUDE DEBUSSY. *Pelléas et Mélisande.* Page 128. (Durand, Pubr.)

Lourd et sombre.

Sen - tez vous l'odeur de mort qui monte

The explanation of passages of this kind must be sought in the sense of the words rather than in the notation of the chords. These may be explained, nevertheless, as unresolved appoggiaturas and as chords of the whole tone scale.

A. BRUNEAU. *Messidor.* Page 179. (Choudens, Pubr.)

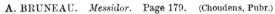

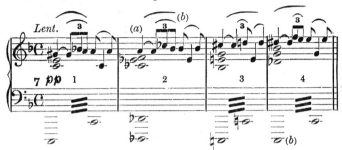

In considering bar 2 separately we have
(b) B♭ appoggiatura of an unheard A♭, that is to say:

but if we consider bars 1, 2, 3, 4, we shall see that the first note is symmetrically the appoggiatura of the harmony note of the 3rd beat:

and we may consider the B♭ as the harmony note, the sixth replacing the 5th, or an anticipation of the 7th.

MAURICE RAVEL. *Gaspard de la nuit.* (*Le Gibet.*) (Durand, Pubr.)

Superimposed fifths.

MAURICE RAVEL. *Miroirs.* (*Alborada.*)   (Demets, Pubr.)

The passage transposed into D♯ minor becomes easy to analyse: (*a*) is simply an inversion of the 9th.

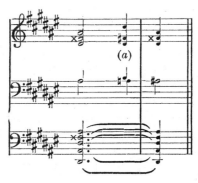

MAURICE RAVEL. *Miroirs (La vallée des Cloches.)*   (Demets, Pubr.)

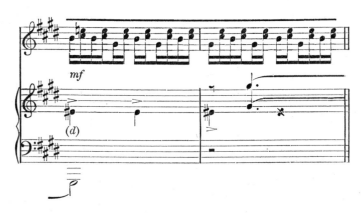

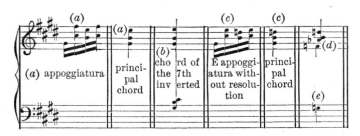

(e) G♮ root of a chord of the 9th by the equisonance of E♯ with F
(d), and A♭, B and D with G♯, B and D.

V. D'INDY.*   *L'Etranger (Introduction to Act II.)*   (Durand, Pubr.)

The most simple combinations are sometimes of great effect. Such is the shake on G–Ab, which with the retardation below causes the following notes to be heard simultaneously.

'V. D'INDY.   *L'Etranger.*   Page 85.   (Durand, Pubr.)

Lent.

* See page 126.

In "horizontal" writing better count of the musical tissue can be taken by isolating the different counterpoints:

V. D'INDY. *L'Etranger.* Page 91. (Durand, Pubr.)

In music on a contrapuntal basis there is no occasion to look for the chords; what should be observed is the movement of the parts, the relation of the simultaneous sounds of which may at certain moments be classed as "chords."

In the present case we believe it to be the intention of the author to consider the bar (*a*) as being formed of counterpoints written round a single chord.

RENÉ LENORMAND. *Le Jardin des bambous.* (Heugel, Pubr.)

(*a*) Common chord with added sixth and added ninth, approached at the distance of a second.

G. FAURÉ. *La bonne Chanson.*   **No. 4.**   (Hamelle, Pubr.)

Allegretto quasi Andante.

Remote tonalities, lightly touching various chords.*

G. FAURÉ. *Pièces brèves.*   (Hamelle, Pubr.)

Allegro moderato.

It is thus, as we have said in the preface, that M. Gabriel Fauré occupies an exceptional place by the turn, full of elegance and of modernism, which he knows how to give to successions of relatively simple chords.

* J. S. BACH. "A Little Labyrinth of Harmony." Works for Organ, Peters' Edition, Vol. IX.

GABRIEL DUPONT. *Les Caresses.* (Heugel, Pubr.)

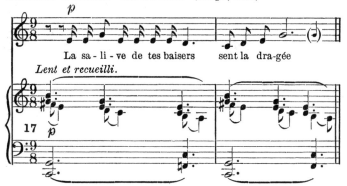

The right hand plays in E minor and the left hand in C major.

GABRIEL DUPONT. *Poèmes d'Automne.* (Astruc, Pubr.)

Chords of the 6th with the bass doubled. The modern flavour obtained by very simple means.

GABRIEL DUPONT. *Poèmes d'Automne.* (Astruc, Pubr.)

Et lan-gou-reu-se-ment la clar-té se re - ti - re: Dou -

très calme.

ceur! Ne plus se voir distincts!N'etre plus qu'un! Silence!

Successions of chords of the 9th of different species in the fourth inversion.

A. ROUSSEL. *Soir d'été.* (*3rd part of the Poème de la Forêt.*)

(Rouart & Lerolle, Pubr.)

Explanation:

(*a*) Chord of the tonic of Db minor with the sixth added.
(*b*) 3rd inversion of the chord of the dominant 9th with the 5th altered, on Cb dominant of Fb.
(*c*) Chord of the dominant 7th of Db understood.
(*d*) Eb pedal, or merely a foreign note to the first chord.

A. ROUSSEL. *Forêt d'hiver.* (Rouart & Lerolle, Pubr.)

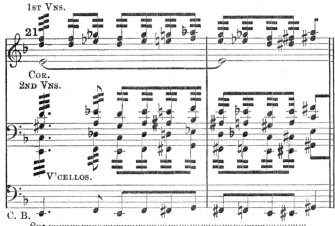

Successions of chords of the ninth (by conjunct degrees) the sixth replacing the 5th. The minor 6th being identical with the augmented 5th, the passage may be analysed as chords of the 9th with upward alteration of the 5th, the whole on an inner pedal.

A. ROUSSEL. *Résurrection.* (Rouart & Lerolle, Pubr.)

(*a*) Chord of the dominant 9th with appoggiatura.
(*b*) Eb appoggiatura of the 5th.
(*c*) Chord of the diminished 7th of the key of G minor.
(*d*) Tonic chord of G minor.

A. ROUSSEL. *Evocation.* (*No. 3.*) (Durand, Pubr.)

A chord built up gradually by its notes being held one after the other and embracing in its full extent the different sounds of the harmonic series.

E. MORET. *Vers tout ce qui fut toi.* (*Pour toi.*) (Heugel, Pubr.)

Et que j'ouvr à ge-noux pour voir comme un tré-

sor   Tout mon pas-sé dans l'ombre é-tin-celer en - cor

This composer often uses the enharmonic notation.

E. MORET. *Une heure sonne au loin.* (*Pour toi.*) Heugel, Pubr.)

(*a*) B appoggiatura of A (*d*).
(*b*) D appoggiatura of the ornamental C♯.
(*c*) Ornamentation of the appoggiatura.
(*d*) A, harmony note (9th in the chord of the 9th on G♯).

E. MORET. *Tubéreuse.* (Heugel, Pubr.)

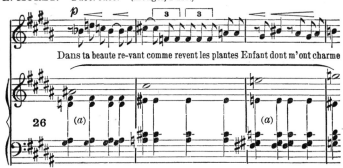

Major 9th without leading note, with downward alteration of the 5th.

CH. KŒCHLIN.   *L'Astre rouge.*   (Rouart & Lerolle, Pubr.)

(*a*) Chord of the 9th on a passing tonic.

CH. KŒCHLIN.   *Accompagnement.*   (Rouart & Lerolle, Pubr.)

Lent et très lié.

(*a*) Chord of the 7th with two appoggiaturas, A♭, C♭.
(*b*) Chord of the 13th formed by the superposition of six thirds.
(*c*) Chord of the 7th with A♭ doubled in the lower octave on E♭ pedal.
(*d*) Pedal E♭.

CH. KŒCHLIN. *Rhodante.* (Rouart & Lerolle, Pubr.)

ét sou - dain se-soulève à de-mi, pâle et   som - bre

(*a*) Chord of the 7th on double pedal, A, E. }
(*b*) Chord of the 7th on double pedal Ab, Eb. } Chords having no tonal significance and written solely for their sonority and the relation which they have to the words.

CH. KŒCHLIN. *L'astre rouge.* (Rouart & Lerolle, Pubr.)

poco allarg. a tempo. (un peu ralenti).

The simplicity of the original harmonies of this passage is surprising.

LOUIS AUBERT.   *Odelette.*   (Durand, Pubr.)

Et c'est ton   om - bre que je cher- che

(a) The voice employs the notes constituting the chord of $\frac{7}{4}$ on F of the first bar.
(b) Appoggiatura.
(c) Quadruple appoggiatura of the chord of C (d).
(e) B♮ for C♭.

LOUIS AUBERT.   *Préludes.*   (*Crépuscule d'Automne.*)   (Durand, Pubr.)

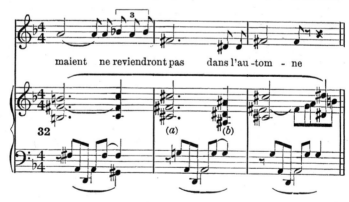

maient   ne reviendront pas   dans l'au -tom - ne

(a) Chord of $\frac{7}{4}$ on A (on pedal D) F♯ appoggiatura.
(b) Double unresolved appoggiaturas:

LOUIS AUBERT. *Nuit mauresque.* (Durand, Pubr.)

These bars, and the whole phrase that follows, rest on the chord of $^9_7$ on B♭. The alterations of F (F♭), and of C (C♭) are unvarying and unresolved, giving the scale

PAUL DUKAS. *Ariane et Barbe-Bleue.* (Durand, Pubr.)

(*a*) Chords of the augmented 5th proceeding by step.
(*b*) Chord of ^{7} on F with altered 5th in the 3rd inversion. The E♭ afterwards becomes a pedal.
(*c*) Several interpretations are possible for the intermediate chords. The best would be to consider them as formed of melodic notes of different kinds.

PAUL DUKAS.   *Ariane et Barbe-Bleue.*   (Durand, Pubr.)
    page 102.

Mon long baiser de sœur vous a-t-il fait du

Passage comprised in the chord of $\frac{9}{7}$ on C♯  with the
5th altered (F✕ for G♮).

Harmony notes:

The other notes are appoggiaturas without resolution, or passing
notes.   The B♯ of the voice is borrowed for the melodic line from the
passing notes of the orchestra.

JEAN HURÉ.   *Sonate pour Piano et Violoncelle.*   (F♯ minor, 1904.)
                                                  (Mathot, Pubr.)

Example of a melody accompanied by modern harmonies. This sonata, from the point of view of the equipoise between a melody of straightforward progression and an extremely modern harmony, is worthy of note. See Chap. XII, Conclusion, page 140.

JEAN HURÉ. *Sonate pour Piano et Violoncelle.* (F♯ *minor.*)
(Mathot, Pubr.)

This fragment is readily explained by reference to Chapter **X**, (Whole tone scale).

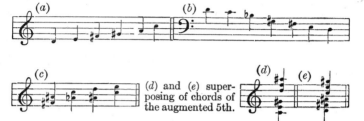

(d) and (e) super-
posing of chords of
the augmented 5th.

(See Whole-tone scale harmonized.)

JEAN HURÉ.   *Suite sur des chants Bretons.*   (1898.)   (Mathot, Pubr.)
For Piano, Violin & 'Cello.

The chord (a) may be analysed in two ways:
1. B♭ appoggiatura of A♭ not heard,
in a chord of the augmented 6th on A♭.

2. By taking F♯ as G♭, the chord
of the 9th on A♭ is formed.

JEAN HURÉ.   *Sonata in F major.*   (1906.)   (Mathot, Pubr.)
For Piano & Violoncello.

Allegro ma non troppo.

The bars 1, 3 and 4 are formed of the chord of F with the 6th added; all the foreign notes are passing notes or ornamentations:

Bar 2, chord of the 9th on D♭; B♭ ornamentation:  Bar 5, chord of the 9th on G♭; E♭ appoggiatura of F♭ or of the unheard D♭.

The harmonies simply stated are:

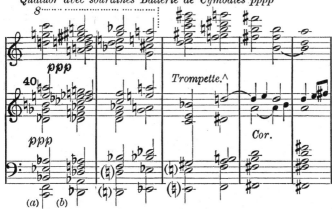

JEAN HURÉ. *La Cathedrale.* (Drama in preparation.) (1910–1912.)
Quatuor avec sourdines Batterie de Cymbales pppp

M. Jean Huré has communicated to us this unpublished fragment, which defies analysis. The chords come without doubt into the category of those written for their sonority without regard to musical grammar (?).

We observe only that in the chords (*a*) and (*b*) the same notes are heard under different conditions in changing octaves, and that the chord (*a*) sounds *all the notes* of the chromatic scale.

M. FAURÉ.   *Le parfum impérissable.*   (J. Hamelle, Pubr.)
Andante molto moderato.

Mon cœur est embau - mé d'une odeur immortel - le. . .

The close of each strophe really ought to be quoted.   Moreover, the whole melody deserves to be cited as a most typical example of refined and modern expression.

ERIK SATIE.   *Le fils des étoiles.*   (Rouart & Lerolle, Pubr.)
Wagnérie Kaldéenne du Sar Péladan.   (1891..)

Prelude to 1st Act.   Prelude to 2nd Act.
En blanc et immobile.   Dans la tête.

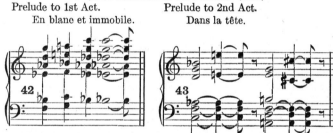

We often hear it said that the modern school, at its beginning, was inspired by Moussorgsky.   If some critics allow that line of descent, several composers affirm that they have found their point of departure in the harmonies of M. Erik Satie.   These harmonies were written twenty or twenty five years ago, in a style independent of all the technical conventions usual at the time.

Prelude to 3rd Act.
Courageusement facile et complaisamment solitaire.

Is it necessary to say that the indications of style apply to the phrases and not to the quoted chords?
This work is written without bar-lines.

We quote these harmonies, leaving the reader to estimate them to his own liking.

ERIK SATIE. *uspud* (1892–93.) *Ballet Chrétien.*
Fragment from 1st Act. (Rouart & Lerolle, Pubr.)

(*a*) These two last chords should be read in the G clef. According to a note by the author, this conventional style of writing has been adopted "to keep away the stupid."

ERIK SATIE. *2nd Sarabande* (1887.) (Rouart & Lerolle, Pubr.)

These harmonies (42) to (47), astonishing for the epoch when they were written, are readily analysed by the means which have served us up to the present.

FANELLI.(*) *Tableaux symphoniques.* (1883.) (Unpublished).
From the Roman de la Momie (TH. GAUTIER.)
1st Part.
Triumphal Entry of Pharoah.
Allegro moderato.

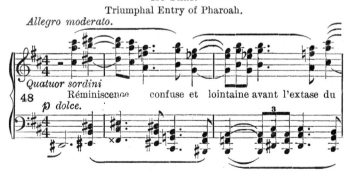

Pharaon   devant   la beauté   de Tahoser, etc.

The lower parts form a succession of diminished 5ths and minor 7ths, proceeding by similar motion in all the parts, and imitating at the 7th the two upper parts. These make a succession of major thirds deriving from the whole tone scale.

"Pharoah" theme.

This passage is based on the whole tone scale.

The quotations from the works of M. Fanelli have a great interest, by reason of the period when these works were written. Composed in 1883, the first part of the "Tableaux Symphoniques" did not become known to the public until 1912!

FANELLI.(*)   *Same Work. 2nd Part*, 1886.
Dans une salle du palais. Jongleuses nues.

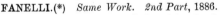

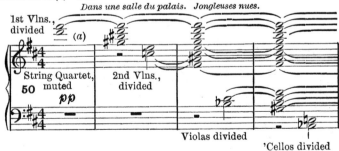

Violas divided

'Cellos divided

---

* M. Fanelli was born in Paris of an Italian father and a Belgian mother. He has always lived in the musical centre of Paris, and, for that reason, may be accounted as one of the French musicians.

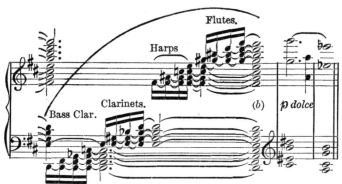

(*a*) The successive entries of the string instruments give a succession of major thirds by whole tones (by leaps of an octave):

(*b*) Chord formed by the superposition of four chords of $\frac{7}{+}$ with altered fifth:

It should be noticed that the last chord G♯, B♯, D♮, F♯ is enharmonically an inversion of the first chord, D♮, F♯, A♭, C♮. By treating the notes enharmonically the chord (*b*) becomes accordingly a chord of the 13th with alterations.

FANELLI.   *Le Cauchemar.*   1888.   (Unpublished).
(Victor HUGO).

(*a*) Chord of the 11th with minor third.

Le monstre volant sur un lac du feu.

etc.

(*a*) Chord of the augmented 11th with altered 5th :

(*b*) Chord of the augmented 11th with altered 7th :

FANELLI. *Impressions pastorales.* 1890. (Unpublished.)

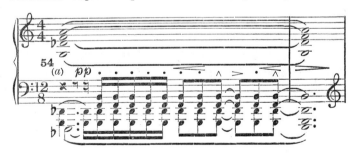

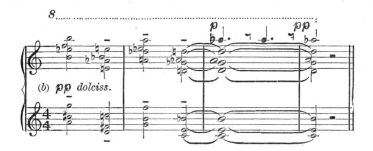

(a) Chord of the augmented 11th.

(b) Chords of the 9th with altered 5th and a 13th added. Progressions by descending 5ths.

VARIOUS DEDUCTIONS AND
REFLECTIONS

Some musicians will see in the harmonic series the in-
dubitable origin of the chords now in use, chords which
their predecessors little by little discovered by intuition.
According to these musicians the origin of these chords may
be established in the manner following, which leads up to
the use of a chord of the augmented eleventh:*

Sounds 1 and 2. Octave.	Sounds 3 and 4. 5th and 4th.	Sounds 5 and 6. Thirds (**) and sixths.
Primitive times.	First centuries of the middle ages.	Close of the 13th century.

Sound 7. 7th.	Sound 9. 9th.	Sound 11. Augmented 11th.
Modern times to the close of the 17th century.		Future and even present time.

* M. Jean Marnold, in the bulletin No. 2 of 1908 of the "Institut
Psychologique," indicates very nearly the same formation of chords.

** The third, which appeared in the 13th century, was used at the
same time as the fifth and the fourth in the Mixed Organum. It was
objected to by reason of its dissonance. Nevertheless, Jean Cotton,
who lived in the 11th century, wrote: "Master Salomon has had sung
the fifth at the same point where Master Albin taught the fourth and
where Master Trudon will allow nothing but the third." That seems
to us to indicate that two hundred years before the date fixed by the
historians, the third, in practice, was used, in the same manner as the
fifth and the fourth.

Attractive as may be the interpretation given to this series of intervals, it is both disputable and disputed.*

Some say, rightly, that the sound 11 is no more an F♯ than the sound 7 is a B♭; others affirm that the formation of the chords by superposition of thirds cannot be accepted, and that the chord of the 11th cannot exist; but their opponents come forward and derive *all* chords from a superposition of thirds.

We leave the theorists to explain it among themselves and say, following M. Marnold, that M. Debussy has used the chord of the augmented 11th in "Pelléas et Mélisande." We have given an example from M. Florent Schmitt (1), and several examples from M. Fanelli (52), (53), (54).

* * *

It is important to notice that the school of which M. Vincent d'Indy is the chief, is also very modern in its manner of treating counterpoint. The means of analysis being different, the examination of the methods in use in modern counterpoint must form a separate task, though on parallel lines with the present. Notwithstanding this we have quoted several passages from M. Vincent d'Indy, because it is impossible to write a work on modern music without naming this eminent composer; his place would be momentous in an analytical study of works characterised more by "horizontal" writing than by "vertical" writing. (12) and (13).

* * *

All the foregoing quotations bear upon harmonic facts typical of modern writing; their character from the point of view of "composition" has not been considered. There is no need to dissimulate the fact that all these peculiarities of writing, interesting in themselves, are nothing if they do not enter into the logical development of a musical thought. Perhaps it may be a reproach to some musicians that they have allowed themselves to be seduced by the search for rare phenomena, to the detriment of inspiration.

We often meet with works so bristling with interesting harmonies that emotion is practically excluded. Here we have a stumbling-block which true musicians will know how to avoid. Moreover, it would be rash to pass judgment on the sincerity of the emotion of modern composers, and a musician who is accused of "gratuitous complication" often only shows a very sincere sensibility, in a form which to him has become familiar and personal.

---

* In the "Principes du Système musical et de l'Harmonie" of **M. Anselme Vinée** (J. Hamelle, Publisher), read his theory of chords.

* * *

New systems develop themselves from different sides.*
Some are based on the harmonic series, others on the division
of the octave into small intervals, while still others bring the
division into twelve equal semitones.   The partisans of this
last division have not failed to notice that modern composers
often write ♯ for ♭ and *vice versa*, as the two notations indicate

---

* We have said in the notes on page 8, that finding his works un-
intelligible, we have scarcely ventured to quote Mr. Schoenberg, of
Vienna.   Two bars from that author will suffice to explain our reserve.
Mr. Schoenberg is a professor at the Conservatoire at Vienna.

ARNOLD SCHŒNBERG.   *Drei Klavier-Stücke.*   (Universal Edition.)
Op. 11, No. 3.

the same sound.   Chap. XI (10), (20), (24), (26); Chap. VI
(4), (8), etc.   Still further, in certain scores may be found
a phrase with sharps in one part, and the same phrase with
flats in another part, moving at the octave, or in unison
with the first.

* * *

It will occur to no one to deny to the older technique the
possibility of chromatic and complicated harmonies.   On
that subject one may re-read Bach, Schumann, Chopin, as
well as Wagner, who by comparison is allied with the older
music rather than with the modern music.   As to Beethoven,
he seems to have concerned himself little with harmonic
research; in the complete power of his genius, he gave
himself to the development of ideas.   This attained such
greatness that the piquancy of uncommon harmonies became
useless.   Nevertheless, he never drew back from any harmonic boldness of which he had need for the interpretation
of his thought.*

---

* We have already quoted the opening of the Finale of the 9th
Symphony (note, page 68).   Here is another example from the Finale
of the "Pastoral" Symphony.   Fètis, as a good professor of harmony,
corrected this passage, "that mistake (!) of a great artist."   This
fragment is usually analysed as an entry of the Horn in the key of C
on a pedal on F.   We cannot refrain from considering the G as a retardation of A.

We quote further the following passage from the 5th Symphony,
which brought against Beethoven the most bitter criticisms on the part
of professors of harmony; —

Composers of classical education may write in modern harmonies,** their technical skill permitting them to attack every variety of form.   Do they then perform this as an act of freewill, or do they involuntarily fall beneath the influence of the atmosphere of to-day?   It is a difficult point to decide.

Besides, in seeking an answer to our question, we may find that certain authors are modern only in their *wish* to write remote harmonies, and are not led to do so by their natural feeling.

Foot-note to p. 137 (cont.)

** THÉODORE DUBOIS.   *Promenade à l'étang.*   (Heugel, Pubr.)

* * *

In this short review of the harmonies employed to-day, we have not been able to quote all composers, and we have not always given to those that we have quoted the important place which is due to them. We have to ask of them all not to see any partisanship in our silence or our reserve. The works available in our library have alone determined the choice of quotations. These have been made in a spirit of entire impartiality, without taking any account of our own preferences.

CHAPTER XII

CONCLUSION

When it is seen that each of the passages quoted may be explained by means of the older technique, the reader may be tempted to conclude that modern harmony is no other than classical harmony treated with greater liberty. This would not be quite exact. Strictly speaking, nearly all the new music can be analysed with the aid of the older treatises on harmony and counterpoint, modern authors having all made classical studies, the minds of the greatest innovators bowing involuntarily to the indelible influence of that teaching. It therefore results that in the most modern music we may nearly always recognise, in spite of dissimilarity, the strand which connects it with the classical technique.

Nevertheless it seems to us that there is in this music a new harmony in a latent condition, which ere long will break that strand, which will throw down the ramparts with which the professors of harmony have involuntarily encircled the ancient teaching.

If we have been able, not without a certain feebleness, to analyse some bars of modern music, artists will be quick to perceive the insufficiency of our commentaries. A new technique is required for modern thought. It will not be formulated, we believe, except by an artist having the power to develop himself outside the schools, and it will depend on the position taken by the theorists with regard to the origin of the notes.

To establish a system we must lean upon something that is stable; but to-day, we are in the presence of three series of notes which, at every instant, mix themselves in a most illogical manner; — Pythagorean notes, natural notes and tempered notes. Choice must be made eventually, and the theory of harmony brought into line with the instruments.

In our preface we examined the different routes which may be followed by composers in a future time. Without taking any side in the question, we may notice that the theoretical division of the octave into twelve equal semitones has nothing illogical about it, seeing that it exists in practice, by the use of the instruments of fixed sounds, and that our composers manifest more and more a kind of indifference in the choice between ♯ and ♭.*

---

* We have found examples of this in our best modern authors, who cannot be taxed with ignorance.

In expressing this opinion we desire to give rise to useful discussion, and have no intention of extolling any new system. Any other technique which will abolish the absurdity of writing a music which cannot be executed, and which will open a wider path for the evolution of to-day, must excite the interest of all musicians.

But, it will be said, this will make it necessary to modify the theory of music! We do not ask for this, but, why should not such change be made? Did the Greek system prevent the theorists of the Middle Ages giving us the hexachordal system? And has this hindered the genesis of our present system?

And do they really imagine that this last must remain to the end of time? This would surely be too naïve.

At the present time, we have, old and young, been "moulded" by a traditional technique, which does not leave us at liberty to invent another. To the musicians of to-morrow belongs the task of building a new musical system responding to the needs of composers' thoughts. The music of to-day will be an excellent preparation. To suppose that melody will disappear in the midst of harmonic complications is, we believe, an error. At first, that complication will exist only for musicians of an incomplete education, and afterwards, we may be certain that the melody will extricate itself as readily from the modern harmonies as it has extricated itself from the harmonies of Schumann and Wagner. These, to a contemporary of Mozart, would pass for veritable ramblings. . . Besides, was not Mozart accused of lack of melody, in spite of the simplicity of his harmonies?

Let modern musicians write but the music of their period* and they will have fulfilled their duty as artists. The example was set them by Schumann, Chopin, Wagner; Liszt, Berlioz, Saint-Saëns, etc., who, at the suggestion of their surroundings, broke the classical moulds in order to formulate a music adequate to their mentality. The musicians of the school of to-day have followed them in this way.

---

* One conceives that the older artists whose efforts were worthy of admiration, but who remained enclosed in the circle of the studies of their youth, must be displeased at seeing a new art brought to birth, an interpreter of a mentality which is no more theirs and which they cannot, or will not, understand. An old composer, of a humorous turn of mind, once said to us: "In my youth, there were two kinds of music, good and bad; the situation was very simple; one stood for one or for the other. Modern composers — men of great talent — have invented a third kind of music: disagreeable music . . . One no no longer knows which side to take."

But if the masters whom we now quote freed themselves from conventional forms, they did not change the musical language in any radical fashion.

On the contrary our modern composers have completely modified the harmonic idiom at the same time as the form.

We may say also that modern works give us impressions of subtlety and charm more often than impressions of power and grandeur. Must we conclude that the technique of which we have quoted so many examples does not lend itself to the construction of powerful and developed works? Certainly not; we could point to compositions of the new school where these qualities are to be met.

This school has just made a great effort to free itself from the past; we must give it time to take advantage of its conquests and to produce the works which we have a right to expect from it. . . .But if this new art be only a refinement of the older art, arrived at the end of its evolution, the perpetual advancement of the art will not be arrested, and we should see new formulas arise of which we cannot at present foresee the character.*

RENÉ LENORMAND.

---

* At the beginning of this study we predicted the coming of new treatises of harmony; since the time when the principal parts of this work were written, new theories of music have made their appearance:
Principes du Systéme musical et de l'Harmonie, by Anselme Vinée.
Traité d'harmonie ultra moderne, by Louis Villermin.
I Moderni orizzonti della tecnica musicale. Teoria della divisione dell'ottava iu partiug uali, Domenico Alaleona (Torio. Fratelli Bocca, pubrs., 1911).

PRINTED IN GREAT BRITAIN BY
LOWE AND BRYDONE (PRINTERS) LTD., LONDON, N.W.10

● Some Interesting Books ●

RENÉ LENORMAND :

A Study of Twentieth Century Harmony Vol. I
(*Harmony in France to 1914*) ... ... **7/6** net

MOSCO CARNER :

Study of Twentieth Century Harmony Vol. II
(*Contemporary Harmony*) ... ... **6/-** net

Of Men and Music (Collected Essays and Articles)
(184 pages) ... ... (*Cloth*) **7/6** net

GREVILLE COOKE :

Art and Reality (An Essay on the Philosophy of
Æsthetics) ... ... (*Paper*) 3/6, (*Cloth*) **4/6** net

RALPH HILL :

Challenges (a Series of Controversial Essays on
Music). With Introduction by John Ireland and an
Envoi by C. B. Rees ... ... **4/-** net

STEWART MACPHERSON :

Form in Music (*With special reference to the design
of Instrumental Music*) ... ... (*Cloth*) **8/6** net

Music and Its Appreciation (*or the Foundations of
True Listening*) ... ... **6/-** net

Melody and Harmony (*In Three Parts, complete with
Analytical Index*) ... ... (*Paper*) 15/-, (*Cloth*) **20/-** net

Studies in the Art of Counterpoint (*Including Double
Counterpoint Canon and Fugue*) ... ... **15/-** net

CH. M. WIDOR :

Technique of the Modern Orchestra (*Translated by
Edward Suddard*) new edition, with *Instructive Appendix*
by Gordon Jacob (218 pages) ... ... **30/-** net

TOBIAS MATTHAY :

Musical Interpretation (*Its Laws and Principles*) ... **10/-** net

J. ALFRED JOHNSTONE :

Rubato : the secret of expression in pianoforte
playing ... ... **4/6** net

London : Joseph Williams Limited
29 Enford Street, Marylebone, W.1